THE ROUGH GUIDE
Website
Directory

ROUGH
GUIDES

www.roughguides.com

Credits

The Rough Guide Website Directory

Text, Layout & Design:
Peter Buckley & Duncan Clark
First edition created by: Angus J. Kennedy
Proofreading: Carole Mansur
Production: Julia Bovis

Rough Guides Reference

Series editor: Mark Ellingham
Editors: Peter Buckley,
Duncan Clark, Daniel Crewe,
Matthew Milton, Joe Staines
Director: Andrew Lockett

Publishing Information

This fifth edition published September 2005 by
Rough Guides Ltd, 80 Strand, London WC2R 0RL
345 Hudson St, 4th Floor, New York 10014, USA
Email: mail@roughguides.com

Distributed by the Penguin Group:
Penguin Books Ltd, 80 Strand, London WC2R 0RL
Penguin Putnam, Inc., 375 Hudson Street, NY 10014, USA
Penguin Group (Australia), 250 Camberwell Road, Camberwell, Victoria 3124, Australia
Penguin Books Canada Ltd, 10 Alcorn Avenue, Toronto, Ontario, Canada M4V 1E4
Penguin Group (New Zealand), Cnr Rosedale and Airborne Roads, Albany, Auckland, New Zealand

Printed in Italy by LegoPrint S.p.A

Typeset in Minion and Myriad to an original design by Duncan Clark & Peter Buckley

A catalogue record for this book is available from the British Library

ISBN 13: 978-1-84353-552-2
ISBN 10: 1-843-53552-1

1 3 5 7 9 8 6 4 2

Contents

contents

Boxed topics

Read this first

Search and find

The Web is huge. Google alone now indexes more than 8 billion pages – that's more than one for each person in the world. This book reviews fewer than one-thousandth of one percent of these, so it should help you cut through the chaff that constitutes so much of the online world. But before proceeding with the directory, here's a quick tutorial about how to find things in the other 99.99% of the Web – including pages which are listed in this book, but which may have moved to a new address since we went to print. We've also included a quick write-up of the Firefox Web browser, a brilliant alternative to Internet Explorer that should greatly improve your online experience.

When a Web address won't work

Some of the addresses in this book will be wrong by the time you try them – not because we're hopeless, but because they change. That's the way of the Net. But just because a page won't display, that doesn't mean you won't be able to track it down.

When a page won't display, the first thing to do is work out where the problem lies. First **check your connection** by trying another site that's very unlikely to be unavailable (such as www. google.com). If that works, you know it's not your connection that's causing the problem, and you can continue to try and locate the correct address (read on); if no pages will open, you'll need to locate the problem (see below).

When no sites will open

If you can't connect to any website, close and then reopen your browser. It might only be a software glitch. Otherwise, it's most likely a problem with your Net connection or proxy server, if you're using one.

Check your mail. If that fails, disconnect and reconnect to the Net. Check it again. If your mail program connects and reports your mail status normally, you know that the connection between you and your ISP is OK. But there still could be a problem between it and the Net or with your proxy server. Check you have the right proxy settings and, if so, make a note of them and try removing them. If it still doesn't work, ring your ISP and see if there's a problem at their end.

Or you could try diagnosing it yourself. To do this, test a known host – say, www.yahoo.com – with a network tool such as Ping or TraceRoute (search Windows or Mac OS Help for more). If this fails, either your provider's connection to the Net is down or there's a problem with your Domain Name Server. Get on the phone and sort it out.

If you've verified that all connections are open but your browser still won't find any addresses, then the problem must lie with your browser setup. Check its settings, reboot your computer, and try uninstalling and reinstalling the program. Alternatively, try another browser (see p.xx).

When one address won't work

There are various reasons why you wouldn't be able to access a specific webpage. But very often there are steps you can take to access the information you're after. You'll probably be able to work out what the problem is by looking at exactly what happens – such as the error message that your machine may flash up. Here's a run-through of the most likely symptoms you'll encounter.

▶ **Symptom:** An error message saying "File not found – 404 error", or you get directed to another page within the site in question that tells you something like "The page you requested cannot be found".

▶ **Problem:** The host you are trying to access is responding, but the specific webpage you are trying to access isn't there. It has probably been moved or removed. If www.roughguides.com/boguspage.html brought up this message, for example, you'd know the /boguspage.html section was the problem.

▶ **Solution:** If you typed the address in manually, make sure you did it correctly – including uppercase or lowercase letters. Still no luck? Refer below to "Finding that elusive page" (p.xi).

read this first

▶ **Symptom:** An error message saying "The server cannot be found", "The page cannot be displayed" or "DNS lookup error".

▶ **Problem:** Unless you typed in the address incorrectly, the website you're trying to access probably doesn't exist or is temporarily unavailable. The latter may be due to maintenance on the server where the site lives, or because too many people are trying to access it at once.

▶ **Solution:** Check the address, and try adding or removing the www part of the address (so try http://roughguides.com instead of www.roughguides.com, for example). If not, try later – perhaps even days later – and in the meantime search Google for a cache of the page (see p.xii).

▶ **Symptom:** A page or frame instantly comes up blank.

▶ **Problem:** Your browser hasn't tried to fetch the page.

▶ **Solution:** Hit "Refresh". If that doesn't work, reboot your browser and re-enter the address. Failing that, clear your Temporary Internet Files or cache. If you're still having problems and it appears to be related to Internet Explorer security – such as the acceptance of an ActiveX control at an online banking site – check your security settings within Internet Options/Preferences, disable Content Advisor and consider adding the site to your Trusted Sites.

▶ **Symptom:** You can reach a webpage on another computer but not your own.

▶ **Problem:** Your Windows Hosts file could be the problem – especially if you've ever installed any browser acceleration software.

▶ **Solution:** Get rid of the offending acceleration program via "Add/

Remove" in the Windows Control Panel. Then locate the file called Hosts in your Windows folder (it will have no file extension). Open it with Notepad and remove any lines not starting with # except for the localhost entry. Save the file and exit.

▶ **Symptom:** An error message saying "Not authorized to view this page", or words to that effect.

▶ **Problem:** Some sites, or files within sites, require a password to be accessed, or can only be reached from certain systems, such as from a company network.

▶ **Solution:** Train to be a hacker.

▶ **Symptom:** Everything looks weird.

▶ **Problem:** It could be that the web designer hasn't tested the site on more than one browser. Some sites, for example, look fine on Explorer but are badly coded and won't display properly on any other.

▶ **Solution:** Try viewing the page through another browser.

Finding that elusive page

If you can connect to the host (the website) but the individual page isn't there, there are a few tricks to try. Check capitalization, for instance: book.htm instead of Book.htm. Or try changing the file name extension from .htm to .html or vice versa (if applicable). Then try removing the file name and then each subsequent directory up the path until finally you're left with just the host name. For example:

www.roughguides.com/old/Book.htm
www.roughguides.com/old/book.htm

read this first

www.roughguides.com/old/Book.html
www.roughguides.com/old/book.html
www.roughguides.com/old
www.roughguides.com

In each case, if you succeed in connecting, try to locate your page from whatever links appear.

Using a search engine

If you haven't succeeded, there's still hope. Try **searching for the problematic address in Google** (www.google.com), and you may find that, though the actual page is no longer available, you can still access Google's **cached copy** – if so, a link saying "cache" will appear under the search result. You could even use the shortcut, searching for:

cache:www.roughguides.com/old/Book.htm

If that doesn't work, you could try searching in the relevant domain (website) for a keyword from the name of the file or from what you expect the file to contain. So, continuing the above example, you could search with Google for:

Book.htm site:roughguides.com

Also remember that you can use a search engine to look only within URLs (addresses). So if the elusive page has an unusual name, let's say worldcupstats.html, you could search the Web for URLs containing that term. At Google you would enter:

inurl:worldcupstats.html

Get sidetracked

If everything else fails, try searching on related subjects, or scanning through relevant sections of **Yahoo!** or the **Open Directory**.

By this stage, even if you haven't found your original target, you've probably discovered half a dozen similar (if not more interesting) pages, and in the process figured out how to navigate the Net more effectively.

Troubleshooting your browser

Like all other programs, Web browsers occasionally freeze or "crash". This is much less of a problem than it was a few years ago, but it still happens. The first thing to try, when any program stops responding, is the **three-fingered salute**: in Windows hold down the **Ctrl+Alt+Del** keys; on a Mac, press **Apple+Alt+Esc**. This should bring up a dialog box listing all your currently open programs. Select the entry for the misbehaving browser and press "End task" or "Force quit". Once you've confirmed your decision, this should close the browser. If that doesn't help, in Windows try doing the same with the Explorer entry. If everything's still frozen, and your computer won't even switch off, force-reboot your machine by holding down the power button for five seconds.

tip

If your browser or connection is doing anything strange, try looking for a relevant setting that might be causing the problem. On a PC, Internet Explorer's settings lurk under a selection of tabs and buttons in Internet Options, under the Tools menu. On a Mac with Safari, look under Preferences (in the Safari menu) and also the Network section of System Preferences.

Update, scan, reinstall

If your browser continues to give you grief, empty its history and cache (aka Temporary Internet Files). If that doesn't work, use Windows Update (PC) or Software Update in the Apple menu (Mac) to get updates for your system and/

or browser, and also scan your computer for **spyware** and **viruses**. Still no joy? You could try uninstalling and reinstalling the browser – in Windows do this via "Add/Remove" Software in the Control Panel; on a Mac, delete the relevant file in Applications. Alternatively, look online for support…

Internet Explorer Support www.microsoft.com/windows/ie/support
IE Infosite www.ieinfosite.co.uk
Firefox Help www.mozilla.org/support/firefox
Safari Support www.apple.com/support/safari

A quick Gootorial

The art of finding things online quickly and efficiently is, without doubt, a life-changing skill. Google (www.google.com) has made this much easier. Bang almost anything in this powerful search engine and you'll probably get a decent selection of relevant results. Still, you can find things more quickly – and more successfully – if you learn how to take advantage of the many ways that Google offers to enhance your search. Following is a quick example to show you the basics; then, over the page, you'll find a summary of the most useful Google tips and tricks.

A typical search

Suppose we want to search for something on the esteemed author, Angus Kennedy. A few years ago, if you entered angus kennedy into a search engine, you'd get a list of pages that contained the words "angus" or "kennedy", or both. Fine, but it meant you'd get loads of pages about Angus cattle and JFK. These days, most search engines look for pages containing both words.

Unfortunately, there's no guarantee that the two words will be found next to each other. What we really want is to **treat them as a phrase**. A simple way to do this is to enclose the words within quotes: "angus kennedy"

Now we've captured all instances of Angus Kennedy as a phrase, but since it's a **person's name** we should maybe look for Kennedy, Angus as well. However, we want to see pages that contain *either* of these terms. We can do this by inserting an uppercase "OR" between the terms. So let's try this:

"angus kennedy" OR "kennedy angus"

By now we should have quite a few relevant results, but they're bound to be mixed up with lots of irrelevant ones. So we should narrow the search down further and exclude some of the excess, such as pages that contain a different person with the same name. Our target writes books about French literature, so let's start by getting rid of that pesky Rough Guider. To **exclude** a term, place a minus sign (-) in front of it. Let's ditch him, then:

"angus kennedy" OR "kennedy angus" - "rough guide"

A slightly tortuous example, perhaps. But it gives you the idea.

Think logically

To increase your search success and efficiency, think logically about an **exact phrase** that might appear on a target page. This makes finding facts and other specific things incomparably quicker and easier. Making a simple phrase with "is", "was" or another short word will often do the trick.

Let's say you want to find an alternative for the network software NetStumbler but you don't know of any. Instead of just searching for NetStumbler and browsing through hundreds of mostly useless results, try entering **"NetStumbler or"**.

Another example: you've heard a techie friend talking about a "wiki" but you don't quite understand what a wiki actually is. Instead of searching for wiki, which will bring up plenty of incomprehensible results, simply search for the phrase **"a wiki is"**.

Google search wizardry: a guide

Though Google is the world's most popular search engine, most of its users don't make the most of its many special commands. So here's a tutorial in the finer points of Google searching. It may just change your life…

BASIC SEARCHES

Googling: **thomas clark**
> finds pages containing both the terms "thomas" and "clark".

Googling: **"thomas clark"**
> finds pages containing the exact phrase "thomas clark".

Googling: **thomas OR clark**
> finds pages containing either "thomas", "clark" or both.

Googling: **thomas -clark**
> finds pages containing "thomas" but not containing "clark".

All these commands can be mixed and doubled up. So, for example:

Googling: **"thomas clark" OR "tom clark" -economist**
> finds pages containing *either* name but not the word "economist".

FIND A SYNONYM

Use ~ before a word to search for synonyms and related words. For example:

Googling: **~mac**
> will find pages containing "macintosh" and "Apple" as well as "mac".

FIND A DEFINITION

Googling: **define:calabash**
> finds definitions from various sources for the word "calabash". (You can also get to a definition (from www.dictionary.com) of a search term by clicking the link in the right of the top blue strip on the results page.)

FIND A FLEXIBLE PHRASE

Use an asterisk as a substitute for any word in a phrase. For example:

Googling: **"tom * clark"**
> finds "tom frederick clark" as well as just "tom clark".

SEARCH FOR A PAGE THAT NO LONGER EXISTS

Let's say you visit www.roughguides.com, a page you looked at the other day so you know it exists, but, to your horror, it doesn't seem to be there. Fear not, Google probably has a copy.

Googling: **cache:www.roughguides.com**
> finds Google's "cached" (saved) snapshot of the page, if it has one. (You can reach the same page by searching for **www.roughguides.com** and then clicking the "cache" link underneath the relevant result.)

SEARCH WITHIN A SPECIFIC SITE

Use the **site:** command to search within a specific website. This usually gives more, better and more clearly presented results than the site's internal search would (if it has one at all). For example:

Googling: **site:www.guardian.co.uk "thomas clark" OR "tom clark"**
> finds pages containing either version of Thomas Clark's name within the website of *The Guardian* newspaper.

SEARCH URLS (WEB ADDRESSES)

The commands **inurl:** and **allinurl:** let you specify that some or all of your search terms appear within the address (url) of the page. This can be very useful if you remember only part of a web address you want to revisit. It's also good for limiting your search to certain types of website. For example:

Googling: **"arms exports" inurl:gov**
> finds pages containing the phrase "arms exports" in the webpages with the term gov in the address (ie, government websites).

SEARCH TITLES

intitle: and **allintitle:** let you specify that one or all of your search terms should appear in the title of a webpage (the text that appears on the top bar of your browser window when viewing a page). This can be useful if you're getting lots of results that mention your terms but don't specifically focus on them. For example:

Googling: **train bristol intitle:timetable**
> will find pages with "timetable" in their titles, and "train" and "bristol" anywhere in the page.

read this first

NUMBER AND PRICE RANGES

Google lets you search for a range of numbers – especially useful for dates. You can also search for a range of prices, though at the time of writing, only the dollar sign can be used.

Googling: **1972..1975 "snooker champions"**
> finds pages containing the term "snooker champions" and any number (or date) in the the range 1972–1975. Googling **numrange:1972-1975** has the same effect.

Googling: **$15..30 "snooker cue"**
> finds pages containing the term "snooker cue" and any price in the range $15–30. Googling **pricerange:15-30** has the same effect.

SEARCH SPECIFIC FILE TYPES

The command **filetype:** lets you specify that your search terms should appear in a specific file, such as pdf format. For example:

Googling: **filetype:pdf climate change statistics**
> would find pdf documents (likely to be more "serious" reports than web pages) containing the terms "climate", "change" and "statistics".

FIND LINKING PAGES

Links are usually one-way: you can see links from a page, but not links *to* a page. In Google, though, you can find out. For example:

Googling: **link:www.roughguides.com/music/index.html**
> finds pages which have a link to the Rough Guides' music homepage.

CALCULATIONS AND CONVERSIONS

OK, so it's not exactly searching, but Google can act as an excellent calculator. It can cope with standard mathematical functions – such as * (multiply), / (divide), + (add), - (subtract) and ^ (raise to the power) – as well as hundreds of units of measurement, from Fahrenheit to hectares. For example:

Googling: **3465*34223**
> will give you the answer 118,582,695.

Googling: **(24-9)% of (36^4 - 3)**
> will give you the answer 251,941.95.

Googling: **51 Fahrenheit in Celsius**
> will give you the answer, 10.55 degrees Celsius.

Googling: **5 gallons in teaspoons**
   will give you the answer "5 US gallons = 3840 US teaspoons"!

IMAGES AND OTHER SPECIAL SEARCHES

Besides images, groups and news searches, Google can also do searches focusing on Apple Macs, Linux and Microsoft. Just click on Advanced Search.

REGIONAL GOOGLE

If you're outside the US, don't forget to use your regional branch of Google so you have the option to search only pages from your country.

AND MORE...

Though they're mostly limited to the US, Google can retrieve relevant information if you search for a **flight number**, an express **delivery tracking number**, a **vehicle ID number** and many other such things.

   For a full list of Google tools and shortcuts, see www.google.com/help. And if you don't fancy remembering the special commands listed above, many of them can be inputted via a form on Google's Advanced Search page.

   Or for answers about every Google-related question you could ever want to ask, see www.geocities.com/googlepubsupgenfaq, the comprehensive FAQ from google.public.support.general newsgroup. More Google news, views, gossip, tips, history and the rest at:

Elgoog www.elgoog.nl
Unofficial Google Weblog http://google.weblogsinc.com

Welcome at Elgoog.nl, an ode to Google
This Google info page about
Elgoog,Googlemania,google,pageranking,groups,dance,tools,filtering,add,url,viewer,logo's,adwords,answers,
froogle,compute,dance,toolbar,forums,blogs,tools,api's,francais,deutsch,seo,toolbar,searchengine,zoeken,zoek,nederlands

Links to/from Google itself
Sitemap, Google Add Urls Google viewer...

More Google's
Domains, Fake and Parody...

Googlemania
Funny logo's, Google history...

Other Google services
Adwords-Answers, Froogle-Compute...

Pageranking
Pagerank, Toolbar...

Groups
Forums, Blogs...

Google in articles
Persons-Research, News-articles...

The Dance
Dance check tool, Dance 2002 pictures...

Tools
Api's, Ip adresses...

Filtering
Germany, China...

Links in other languages
Deutsch German, Francais French...

Oldindex
Other Searchengines, SEO...

Bin Explorer, get Firefox

If you have a PC, the chances are you'll be looking at the sites listed in this book through Microsoft's **Internet Explorer**, aka **IE** – the Web browser that comes built into the Windows operating system. The current version of IE is decent enough, but it certainly isn't the best browser available. It lacks many of the useful features of some alternatives, and it's widely considered to present problems in terms of security. For both these reasons – and because Microsoft is probably not a company you're desperate to support – you should at least test-drive something else, the obvious choice being Firefox…

Firefox

Released in late 2004, Firefox is a superb browser created by the Mozilla Foundation with the help of volunteer programmers around the world. Released as an open-source product, Firefox has a huge range of features, and even if you discover something that it can't do you'll often find that you can easily add the desired function via an extension (look in the Tools menu) or some other customization. There are extensions available for everything from blocking banner ads to translating text into different languages.

Firefox is also very secure, leaving PC users less vulnerable to potentially harmful scripts and other Web-based nasties than Internet Explorer does. With a built-in Google search box, customizable address-bar searching, excellent privacy tools, tabbed browsing and many other handy extras, Firefox is an essential free download for PC users – and well worth exploring for Mac users, too. Try it out by dropping by:

Firefox www.getfirefox.com

The Directory

The Directory

The best of the Web

Amusements

Looking for a chuckle or perhaps to extend your lunchbreak into the late afternoon? Click through the following directories to enter a whole new dimension of time-wasting:

Ranks.com www.ranks.com/home/fun/top_humor_sites
Open Directory http://dmoz.org/Recreation/Humor
Yahoo! http://dir.yahoo.com/Entertainment/Humor

If you have a high-bandwidth connection or are blessed with abnormal patience, you might like to investigate the world of online animation. Offerings range from clones of old-school arcade games to feature-length Flash cartoons. Peruse the galleries and links from:

About Animation http://animation.about.com
Animation http://dmoz.org/Arts/Animation
b3ta www.b3ta.com
David Shrigley www.mudam.lu/shrigley
Flasharcade www.flasharcade.com

amusements

Flashgames www.theflashgames.com
Flashkit www.flashkit.com
Flazoom www.flazoom.com
Shockwave www.shockwave.com

Ali G Translator
www.webdez.net/alig
Make yourself comprehensible to the Staines massive.

Assassin
www.newgrounds.com/assassin
Waste a few excess celebrities.

Brain Candy
www.corsinet.com/braincandy
Riddles, jokes, insults and general wordplay.

Caption of the Day
www.cdharris.net/dailypics
Prepare for your upcoming appearance on *Have I Got News For You*.

Cartoon Bank
www.cartoonbank.com
Every cartoon ever published in *The New Yorker*.

Colouring Book
www.geek-boy.com/colorbook.html
For when you really have nothing better to do.

Comedy Central
www.comedycentral.com
Download full *South Park* episodes, listen to comedy radio and see what's screening across the network. More of a station promo than a source of laughs.

Comic Book Resources
www.comicbookresources.com
A great place to start when looking for comic and cartoon sites and shops. If you're really serious about your comics, check out

Sequential Tart, a webzine about the industry, and these others:
www.sequentialtart.com
www.cartoon-links.com
www.crimeboss.com
www.geocities.com/mbrown123
www.reallifecomics.com

Complaint Letter Generator
www.pakin.org/complaint
Punch in a name for an instant dressing-down.

Computer Pranks
www.computerpranks.com
Convince your friend that his new laptop is possessed.

Cool Optical Illusions
www.coolopticalillusions.com
A nice collection of classic illusions and many more optical oddities
that'll make you say "'cool".

Dean & Nigel Blend In
www.deanandnigel.co.uk
Witness the gentle art of urban camouflage.

amusements

Exorcist Bunnies
www.angryalien.com/0204/exorcistbunnies.html
It's short, it's sharp, it's scary and it's got bunnies in it – what more
do you want?

The Flash Mind Reader
www.flashpsychic.com
Be amazed. Be very amazed.

The Frown
www.thefrown.com
Bitter and twisted cartoons.

Gary Duschl's Gumwrapper Chain
www.gumwrapper.com
If only you had so much ambition.

Graffiti The Web
www.yeahbutisitart.com/graffiti
Vandalise websites for fun.

Guimp
www.guimp.com
The world's smallest fully
featured website?

Half Bakery
www.halfbakery.com
Questionable concepts.

Horrorfind
www.horrorfind.com
A helpful hand into the
darkness.

Hot or Not?
www.hotornot.com
Post a picture of yourself
or someone else, and pass-

ing chumps will rate your attractiveness on a scale of one to ten. So popular it's spawned a plethora of similar sites where you can rate everything from goths to architecture:
www.archibot.com/ratings
www.ratemyface.com
www.gothornot.com
www.amiannoyingornot.com
www.amigeekornot.com

I Love Bacon
www.ilovebacon.com
Most of the gags that arrive in your inbox courtesy of your caring friends will wind up in these, or similar, archives sooner or later. Usually before you see them. Don't go near the galleries if you're a bit sensitive.
www.collegehumor.com
www.mrjoker.net
www.goofball.com

In the 70s
www.inthe70s.com
Re-enter the landscape that wallpapered your childhood memories; and if you are a little younger than that, try one of these:
www.inthe80s.com
www.inthe90s.com

The Insanity Test
www.knplogic.co.uk/are_u_mad.html
Try not to laugh.

Internet Conspiracy Generator
www.westword.com/extra/conspire.html
Are you really that desperate for pub conversation fodder?

The Internet Squeegee Guy
www.website1.com/squeegee
Your monitor's looking a bit dusty.

amusements

Japanese Engrish
www.engrish.com
Copywriters wanted, English not a priority.

Jester: the Online Joke Recommender
http://shadow.ieor.berkeley.edu/humor
It knows what makes you laugh.

Joke Index
www.jokeindex.com
So many jokes it's not funny. And there's loads more to be found
here, here, here, here and here:
www.humor.com
www.humordatabase.com
www.humournet.com
www.looniebin.com
www.twistedhumor.com

Mini Pool
www.fetchfido.co.uk/games/minipool/minipool.htm
Play against the clock to clear the table.

National Lampoon
www.nationallampoon.com
Daily humour from the satire house that PJ built. Not what it was in
the 1970s, as you'll see from the vault.

The Official Rock-Paper-Scissors Strategy Guide
www.worldrps.com
Master such techniques as Speed Play, Rusty and Lowball, then make
like Gary Kasparov and play the computer.

The Onion
www.theonion.com
Unquestionably the finest news satire on or off the Net. See also:
www.private-eye.co.uk
www.satirewire.com
www.spin-on-this.com

Online Etch-A-Sketch
http://babygrand.com/games
It doesn't quite have the tactile wonder of the original game, but it's a whole lot of fun.

Perpetual Bubblewrap
www.urban75.com/Mag/bubble.html
Seconds of fun for the whole family.

Pet Fish
www.petfish.com
Turn your monitor into a virtual fish tank.

Piercing Mildred
www.mildred.com
Tattoo, pierce and scar Mildred to your heart's content – no fuss, no pus.

The Pocket
www.thepocket.com
Gadgets, games, greetings cards, cartoons and more, updated daily.

Pop Cap
www.popcap.com
Loads of games to play online or download. Also see:
www.moonflip.com

The Post-Modernism Generator
www.elsewhere.org/cgi-bin/postmodern
Sprinkle your next essay with "postsemanticist dialectical theory" and fool your teacher.

The Prank Institute
www.prank.org/phpBB2
Mischief for every occasion. Or for a history of hoaxes, visit:
www.museumofhoaxes.com

amusements

Rather Good
www.rathergood.com
See what all the fuss is about. This is one Flash site not to be missed.
Kittens as you've never seen them before playing "Independent
Woman" as you've never heard it before – more fun than you could
have with a tennis racket and a bag of rotten apples.

Rec.humor.funny
www.netfunny.com/rhf
Archives of the rec.humor.funny newsgroup, updated daily.

The Simpsons Zombie Shootout
www.thesimpsons.com/zombie
As you might imagine, *The Simpsons*' website is a great place to kill
some time ... and some zombies.

The Simulator
http://conceptlab.com/simulator
Put yourself in the shoes of a minimum-wage slave at Mackey D's.

Sissyfight
www.sissyfight.com
Scratch, tease and diss your way to playground supremacy.

The Spark.com
www.thespark.com
Most famous for its tests (purity, slut, bastard, etc) which have been taken by some eight million people, plus numerous other ways to laugh at your friends. Find more unreliable information about yourself at Emode at:
www.emode.com

Star Wars Asciimation
www.asciimation.co.nz
The *Star Wars* saga rendered in vivid ASCII text – George Lucas would be spinning in his grave if he were dead.

Stick Figure Death Theater
www.sfdt.com
Stickcity citizens meet their sticky ends.

Superjam
www.super-jam.com
Upload a picture of yourself, paste it on one of the dancing figures and watch yourself do the Smurf.

The Surrealist Compliment Generator
www.madsci.org/cgi-bin/cgiwrap/~lynn/jardin/SCG
"In caressing your follicles I am only vaguely reminded of the bitter harvest", and other bons mots.

UnderGround Online
www.ugo.com
Vigilante gang of counterculture sites – the antithesis of AOL.

Universal Translator Assistant Project
http://hometown.aol.com/JPKlingon/uta
Translate the Bible into Klingon, Vulcan, Romulan – even Esperanto! Of course, you could always just teach yourself Klingon at the

Klingon Language Institute:
www.kli.org

Web Economy Bullshit Generator
www.dack.com/web/bullshit.html
Learn how to "leverage leading-edge mindshare" and "incubate compelling interfaces".

Weird Puppet
www.wiredpuppet.com
Harness the power of Quicktime and make guitar boy dance.

Xiaoxiao
www.xiaoxiaomovie.com
The Jackie Chan and Bruce Lee of the stick-figure world battle to the death. Head straight for "No. 3".

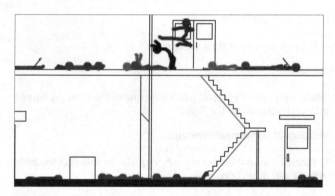

Antiques & Collectables

Action Figure Collectors
www.actionfigurecollectors.com
Looking for that elusive Lando Calrasian toy? Try here first.

Antique Hot Spots
www.antiquehotspots.com
No-nonsense and very comprehensive set of links to online antique dealerships.

Antiques on the Web
www.bbc.co.uk/antiques
The BBC's superb antiques site includes buying advice from *Antiques Roadshow* experts, feature articles, hints on scoring big at car boot sales, exhibition listings and the latest finds from the *Roadshow*.

Antiques UK
www.antiques-uk.co.uk
Similar to most antique portals in that it offers links to dealers and salvage warehouses, but it has an excellent want ads feature – allowing you to post a message if you're after a specific item and a dealer can then get in touch with you through the site.

Antiques Web
www.antiques-web.co.uk
A comprehensive database of directory information (including the best list of UK antiques fairs on the Net) for the British antiques community.

Cartophilic Society of Great Britain
www.csgb.co.uk
Homepage of the organization devoted to card collecting.

Collectics
http://collectics.com/education.html
A variety of essays on collectable antiques covering Clarice Cliff to Lalique.

antiques & collectables

Collecting Airfix Kits
www.djairfix.freeserve.co.uk
A shockingly in-depth site devoted to plastic modelling.

Collector Café
www.collectorcafe.com
A portal for the collecting community, with channels for just about every collectable from advertising memorabilia to writing instruments. For a UK-based portal, try:
www.antiquesbulletin.com
www.antiquesworld.co.uk
www.worldcollectorsnet.com

Comics International
www.comics-international.com
Perhaps the most useful comics site on the Web, this gateway features a near-definitive directory of UK stockists, an excellent links page, comics reviews and unusually informative FAQs. Also see:
http://comicbooks.about.com

I Collector
www.icollector.com
The eBay of the high-end collector's market, this auction site hosts more than 650 auction houses selling everything from Francis Bacon originals to George II armchairs.

Invaluable

www.invaluable.com

If you can't get to the *Antiques Roadshow* or you're a serious collector, the online branch of *Invaluable* magazine provides an appraisal
service. If you've had an item stolen, it also has a tracer service to
improve your odds of recovering it. These don't come cheap, but
you can try them for free. A similar, less expensive service used to
be offered by the American site, Eppraisals, but this has now been
integrated into eBay.

Kitsch

www.kitsch.co.uk

UK site for collectors of retro-chic featuring *Dukes of Hazzard* items,
Presleyana, lava lamps, James Bond paraphernalia, etc. As an added
bonus, they belong to the Which? Webtrader code of practice, so
you know you can buy that Farrah pencil in confidence.

antiques & collectables

Labelcollector.com
www.labelcollector.com
Salute the golden era of fruit crates and jars.

LAPADA
www.lapada2.co.uk/index.html
The homepage of the Association of Art and Antique Dealers features a directory of members, fair and auction listings and advice on buying, selling, taking care and providing security for antiques.

Modern Moist Towelette Collecting
http://members.aol.com/MoistTwl
As opposed to classic moist towelette collecting.

Numismatica
www.limunltd.com/numismatica
With loads of articles, news, listings, FAQs, guides and links, this is the best portal for coin collectors on the Web. For banknote collectors, try Collect Paper Money:
www.collectpapermoney.com

Old Bear
www.oldbear.co.uk
Don't throw away that beat-up, stinky old teddy bear – it might be worth a few sovereigns. This site will tell you if you can start a trust fund with your Gund or if you're stuck for life with your Steiff.

Philatelic Resources on the Web
www.execpc.com/~joeluft/resource.html
Joseph Luft's listing of more than 4000 websites devoted to stamp collecting.

Sandafayre
www.sandafayre.com
Auctions and information from the world's largest stamp dealer.

TV Toys
www.tvtoys.com
One of the best sites to explore the ever-expanding world of TV memorabilia with knowledgeable articles about collecting certain shows and links to collectables for sale.

Watchnet
www.watchnet.com
Online hub for the vintage wristwatch collecting community.

World War II Collectibles
www.wwii-collectibles.com
Lame layout, but beneath the clutter and bad interface lies a treasure trove of stamps, coins, posters, propaganda material and military ephemera.

Architecture

Adam
http://adam.ac.uk
Designed for university students, this is a search engine of Internet resources for art, architecture and design.

Archibot
www.archibot.com
If you're interested in contemporary architecture and design, this very sexy site is the best portal on the Web. It features news and links that are updated daily (you can have them emailed to you),

forums and an excellent metasearch engine to weed out all the building code sites.

Architecture.com
www.architecture.com
For anything relating to British architecture, the Royal Institute of British Architects should be your first port of call. It allows you full access to their database of article abstracts; has a find-an-architect function if you're redesigning your garden shed; and has links to more than a thousand sites.

Architecture Mag
www.architecturemag.com
One of the top online architecture magazines. The others:
www.arplus.com
www.ArchitectureWeek.com
www.metropolismag.com

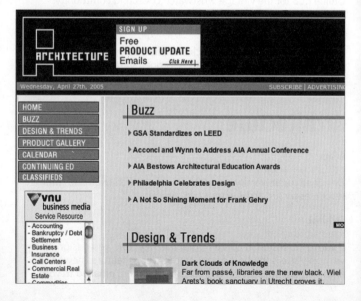

Arcspace

www.arcspace.com

Excellent Danish site devoted to contemporary architecture, with copiously illustrated exhibits, feature articles and portfolios.

Building Conservation

www.buildingconservation.com

Preserve your palace.

Glass, Steel and Stone

www.glasssteelandstone.com

A fun site, with browsable galleries (including ones devoted to haunted and odd architecture), forums and news stories that are updated daily.

Great Buildings Online

www.greatbuildings.com

An exemplary resource. If you download free Design Lite software you can get three-dimensional models of Stonehenge, Chartres Cathedral, Falling Water and other masterpieces by Alvar Aalto, Le Corbusier and Ludwig Mies van der Rohe. Of course, there are also flat photographs and information on the architects of over a thousand great buildings. The constant pop-up ads are very irritating, though.

National Trust

www.nationaltrust.org.uk

The National Trust's site includes information on all of their properties, news, a gift shop and accommodation details.

Art

If you're an artist, photograph your work (preferably with a digital camera) and post it online: it's cheap gallery space and your disciples can visit at any time without even leaving home. But don't expect them to stumble across it randomly. You'll need to hand out its address at every opportunity, and don't forget to include news of your exhibitions and contact details. As in the real world, finding art online is very much a click-and-miss affair (www.glyphs.com/moba), and of course entirely a matter of taste.

If you're looking for online exhibitions turn to the Museums and Galleries section (p.170). The following section is devoted to portals, art education sites, artist resources, etc.

A.A. Art
www.1art.com
For budding Constables, this excellent arts education site offers free online painting lessons, video workshops and forums on technique.

Aliens and UFO Art
www.wiolawapress.com
Defy the Government by becoming as one with alien sculptures.

AllPosters.com
www.allposters.com
Plaster over the cracks in your bedroom walls. Also try Barewalls (www.barewalls.com), but beware of the massive shipping charge on European orders. Also check out:
www.allaboutart.com
www.postershop.co.uk

Amico.org
www.amico.org
Thumbnails from the top North American galleries.

Art Advocate
www.artadvocate.com
Check out and buy work by emerging artists selected by knowledgeable folks from the Big Apple. To buy affordable work from British artists try Art Connection and New British Artists:
www.art-connection.com
www.newbritishartists.co.uk

home   about us   search   events   contact us

Art Capital Group
www.artcapitalgroup.com
Borrow posh pictures to hang in your snooker room.

Art.com
www.art.com
With an address like that, you've got to deliver, and the site does. With its huge catalogue of reproductions, this American site (which ships to the UK) is effectively an art shopping mall.

Art Crimes
www.graffiti.org
The first and still the best graffiti site on the Web. Art Crimes features an amazing array of burners, interviews with the most well-known writers, a good FAQ page and an untouchable set of graf links.

ArtLex
www.artlex.com
This visual arts dictionary is a truly superb resource for students, experts and bluffers alike. Containing extensively cross-referenced definitions of over three thousand terms and examples (reproductions appear either below the definition or are linked to another site hosting one), this is one of the most useful art sites on the Web.

art

Arts councils

For information on everything from National Lottery funding and government grants (they'll only spend it on guns if you don't use it) to online exhibition spaces, this is the first place to check. As well as these national sites there are also click-throughs to even more regional Arts Council websites.

England www.artscouncil.org.uk
Northern Ireland www.artscouncil-ni.org
Wales www.ccc-acw.org.uk
Scotland www.sac.org.uk

Art Net
www.artnet.com
With its frighteningly comprehensive artists' index, excellent exhibition listings and articles both breezy and dense, the homepage of Art Net magazine probably serves as the best art portal on the Web.

D'Art
http://dart.fine-art.com
A giant online art marketplace with more than five thousand participating sites and tens of thousands of works.

Grove Dictionary of Art Online
www.groveart.com
Freeload for a day on the definitive work of art reference.

Interactive Collector
www.icollector.com
Bid for art and collectables such as celebrity cast-offs. Then, of course, there's always eBay (www.ebay.co.uk).

Roadside Art Online
www.interestingideas.com/roadside/roadside.htm
Links page to such delights as the world's largest catsup bottle, Route 66 motel signs, art environments and Pancakes Across America.

World Wide Arts Resources
www.wwar.com
Its URL may lead you to believe that this is a site for military enthusiasts, but this list bank is probably the most comprehensive art
search engine, with links to just about everything from art supplies
and atelier services to gallery spaces and arts education courses.
Also worth a gander is:
www.artcyclopedia.com

Asian Interest

British Born Chinese
www.britishbornchinese.org.uk
Articles, humour, links, a newsletter and more for the British Chinese
population.

Click Walla
www.clickwalla.com
Probably the most wide-ranging site serving Britain's Asian community, Click Walla comprises sections devoted to music, film, news,
students, weddings, food, listings, beauty and fashion, health and
Asian businesses. Other UK portals worth checking out include:
www.redhotcurry.com

India Abroad
www.indiaabroad.com
The focus here is largely on the US and Canada, but this huge site is
a model portal in terms of both content and design, with extensive
news coverage, a broad array of channels, immigration advice, in-
depth interviews and shopping facilities.

Lankaweb
www.lankaweb.com
A virtual community for Sri Lankans across the world.

Sada Punjab

www.sadapunjab.com

Devoted to keeping Punjabi culture alive. The site's features include a literature archive of folktales, ghazals and poems; a Punjabi juke-box; an archive of Sikh religious texts; language tutorials; and a magazine. See also Punjab Online and Punjabi Network:

www.punjabonline.com

www.punjabi.net

South Asia Network

www.southasia.net

This portal features the South Asia search engine and serves as a useful gateway to information on Bangladesh, Bhutan, India, the Maldives, Nepal, Pakistan and Sri Lanka.

Tehelka

www.tehelka.com

A very influential Internet newsletter from India, which has had a role in exposing corruption in politics and helped to break cricket's match-fixing scandal.

Auctions

You know how auctions work: the sale goes to the highest bid-der, as long as it's above the reserve price. Or, in the case of a Dutch auction, the price keeps dropping until a buyer accepts. Well, it's the same online. You simply set a starting bid and then leave an instruction to raise it in preset increments (if and when you get outbid) up to a ceiling. If you're the highest bidder when the auction ends, the deal is struck.

Once the deal's been settled, it's up to the buyer and seller to arrange delivery and payment, though both can be arranged through trusted third parties. There are millions of goods for sale in thousands of categories across hundreds of online auctions.

These days most people turn to eBay, the granddaddy of all auction sites, to satisfy their auction needs:

eBay www.ebay.co.uk

It's by far the best site to use, and though the pages may be hectic and distracting, underneath the clutter **eBay** has millions of items for sale. That said, there are a few other general auction sites worth looking at:

Amazon www.amazon.co.uk/auctions
A1 Auctions www.bullnet.co.uk/auctions
BidXS www.bidxs.com
eBid www.ebid.co.uk
QXL www.qxl.com
Wanadoo www.wanadoo.co.uk/auctions

Here are a few more specialist auction sites, mixed in with a handful that you may find useful as you navigate the auction universe:

I Collector
www.icollector.com
Home to over 650 auction houses, this American site aims to be a high-end eBay with an emphasis on art and antiques. One for the serious collector.

Internet Auction List
www.internetauctionlist.com
This portal to the online bidding scene is the most comprehensive auction directory on the Web.

National Fraud Information Center
www.fraud.com
If you're worried about getting swindled by an online auctioneer, this excellent American site has all the information you need to protect yourself.

Priceline

http://travel.priceline.co.uk

This travel giant has added a new twist to the auction game by allowing you to state how much you'd like to pay for airplane tickets, hotels and car rental, then waiting to see if anyone accepts. LastMinute.com offers a similar service:

www.lastminute.com

Sotheby's

www.sothebys.com

You won't find that signed Kylie picture disc here, but if you've got money to burn, sites don't come any classier than this online home of the august auction house. For similar, if not quite so grand, service, try Bonham's or Christie's:

www.bonhams.com

www.christies.com

Vendio

www.vendio.com

Tools and services for the serious online auction seller. Also see:

www.lotwatch.co.uk/tools

www.SpoonFeeder.com

What the Heck

www.whattheheck.com/ebay

Your guide to the bizarre stuff people try to unload on eBay. Want to see the legendary listing of the person who auctioned their kidney for $2.5 million? It's here, as are listings for partially used packs of cigarettes, old toilet paper and all sorts. Alternatively, go to:

http://listings.ebay.com/pool3/plistings/list/all/category1466

Babies & Parenting

Aware Parenting Institute

www.awareparenting.com

A garish site, but an excellent resource for those interested in child-centred parenting.

Babycare Direct
www.babycare-direct.co.uk
Although ordering could be made a lot easier, this is nevertheless
one of the better UK sites specializing in nursery goods. The range of
their stock is very extensive and they offer some good discounts.

BabyCentre
http://www.babycentre.co.uk
Probably the most complete baby site on the Web, with advice on
everything from conceiving to lullaby lyrics to sleep routines to cop-
ing with your kid bursting into tears on a plane.

BabyNamer
www.babynamer.com
Why not give your babe a cutesy name like Adolph? It apparently
means "noble hero". More suggestions to scar it for life at:
www.babynames.com
www.baby-names-meanings.com

Babyworld
www.babyworld.co.uk
The homepage of *Babyworld* magazine offers all the usual chat
rooms, shopping facilities and pregnancy diaries, plus one of the
most detailed health sections around.

Dr Greene
www.drgreene.com
If your baby gets sick and you can't get to a doctor, try paediatrician
Dr Greene for advice.

babies & parenting

Fathers Direct
www.fathersdirect.com
A good site aimed at working dads, with news on the latest child development research, articles on fatherhood by Red Or Dead's Wayne Hemingway and Laurence Llewellyn-Bowen, information on the paternity leave scheme and other parental resources.

Homebirth
www.homebirth.org.uk
Lots of advice for parents choosing to give birth at home, including birth stories and pain relief options as well as recommended books, videos and articles.

Mothers Who Think
www.salon.com/mwt
As with just about everything else on Salon, this section is funny, informative, engaging and well written, and a perfect antidote to all the sites and publications that treat mums as scarcely more intelligent than their babies.

National Childbirth Trust
www.nctpregnancyandbabycare.com
The NCT's official site is a good place to find out about antenatal classes, breast-feeding counsellors, mothers' groups and the NCT's own books on pregnancy and childbirth.

Net Doctor
www.netdoctor.co.uk/children
Certainly among the best UK health sites, Net Doctor's specialist pages are filled with largely jargon-free information for mother and child. The children's health area is particularly useful as it details the symptoms and treatments of common childhood ailments.

Parents.com
www.parents.com
Unlike many sites linked to paper publications, the homepage of the American magazine *Parents* doesn't skimp on online content, and because of its ties to a respected publication, the advice and information is authoritative.

Pregnancy Calendar
www.pregnancycalendar.com
Count down the nine months from conception to birth and get prepared to juggle your life around your new family member. Also see:
www.parentsoup.com
www.parenthoodweb.com

SheilaKitzinger.com
www.sheilakitzinger.com
Sheila Kitzinger is one of the gurus of childbirth. Her site may be a bit too campaigning for some, but beneath the occasionally hectoring tone and ill-advised poetry there's a wealth of information on breast-feeding, water births, home births and other related issues.

UK Parents
www.ukparents.co.uk
A comprehensive parenting e-zine written in plain and largely unpatronizing language, covering pretty much everything from pre-conception to sending the young 'uns off to school.

Betting & Gambling

It's tempting to say that online betting is for those who like that extra added element of risk, but if you stick to well-known bookmakers who've invested heavily in their security systems and avoid the casinos (which are often pretty dodgy and sometimes require you to buy a CD-ROM or download fifteen megabytes of software) you should be fine. To find a bookie, try **Bookies Index** (www.bookiesindex.com) or go straight to one of the big names:

betting & gambling

BlueSQ www.bluesq.com
Coral Eurobet www.eurobet.co.uk
Ladbrokes www.ladbrokes.com and www.bet.co.uk
Littlewoods www.bet247.com
Paddy Power www.paddypower.com
Sporting Index www.sportingindex.com
Tote www.totalbet.com
Victor Chandler www.victorchandler.com
William Hill www.williamhill.co.uk

National Lottery
www.national-lottery.co.uk
It could be you ... but it probably won't be.

Oddschecker
www.oddschecker.co.uk
Useful site that allows you to view the odds that all the bookies are offering, linking directly to their sites so you can place a bet.

The Racing Post
www.racingpost.co.uk
The online home of the venerable tip sheet.

Settle-a-Bet
www.settle-a-bet.co.uk
How to beat the odds.

24 Dogs
www.24dogs.com
Comprehensive, Wembley-owned greyhound resource and betting service. Also see The Dogs:
www.thedogs.co.uk

UK Betting Guide
www.ukbettingguide.co.uk
Pretty comprehensive portal that will give you hundreds of ways of parting with your cash online.

Win 2 Win
www.win2win.co.uk
One of the very few free horseracing tipster services on the Web, it
also has a section devoted to different betting systems.

World of Gambling
www.gamble.co.uk
News, reviews and advice on everything from baccarat to slot
machines.

Black Interest

Africa Online
www.africaonline.com
This bilingual (French) portal features some of the most comprehensive African news coverage on the Web. Also see:
www.africaguide.com
http://allafrica.com
www.africahomepage.org

Black Search
www.blacksearch.co.uk
Search engine and directory for "Black Orientated" sites.

Black Britain
www.blackbritain.co.uk
This site is an extensive gateway to black British culture, with a
friendly, inclusive feel. Also try Black Net:
www.blacknet.co.uk

blogs

Black Information Link
www.blink.org.uk
The 1990 Trust's bulletin board for the UK's black community serves two functions: it provides news, events listings and links; and it serves as a forum for political advocacy.

Black Presence
www.blackpresence.co.uk
A forum and resource for researchers and other people interested in the history of black culture in Britain. Also includes news, features on music and articles on contemporary figures such as Chris Ofili.

Windrush
www.bbc.co.uk/history/community/multicultural/windrush
The BBC's celebration of fifty years of Afro-Caribbean culture in Britain, with a heavy slant towards education: timelines, achievements, first-person remembrances, poetry and a literature guide.

Blogs

Blogs, or weblogs, are essentially diaries – logs of a person's thoughts, what they did, what's interesting them, and news. They are getting a lot of coverage at the moment because they represent one of the latest developments in the Web's democratization of culture: due to their immediacy and their liberation of the means of production, blogs are being hyped as the new publishing revolution. Following are some blogging resources and some of the best blogs on the Web. See also RSS Newsfeeds (p.204).

Adam Curry's Weblog
http://live.curry.com
Blog of former MTV VJ; go straight to the MTV Chronicle for the dirt.

Apparently Nothing
www.apparentlynothing.com
Regular photographic postings and commentary.

Belle de Jour
http://belledejour-uk.blogspot.com
"The diary of a London call girl"; but is it fact or fictional?

Bert – The Evil One
http://neuromantics.net/bert
Not a happy bunny – please excuse his bad language.

Blogger.com
www.blogger.com
Links, news and everything you need to create your own blog.

BlogSearchEngine
http://blogsearchengine.com
In case you hadn't guessed, this is a blog search engine. It also
boasts loads of articles and blog news features.

Boom Selection
http://boomselection.info
The headquarters of the British bootleg mix scene.

The Bunker
http://neuromantics.net/bunker
Pitching itself as "an outboard brain", this is the genius blog of Paul
Cleghorn.

Call Centre Confidential
http://callcentrediary.blogspot.com
The gripping diary of a call centre team leader.

Coolfer
www.coolfer.com
The definitive Big Apple blog, covering "for the most part" music and
the music industry, and, of course, NYC.

The Daily Report
www.zeldman.com/coming.html
Web guru Jeffrey Zeldman dishes up tech advice and links, and the
wickedly funny "If the great movies had been websites".

blogs

The Diary of Samuel Pepys
www.pepysdiary.com
Every day brings an entry from the renowned 17th-century diarist. If
you've missed his exploits to date, there's a "story so far" page.

DAYPOP
www.daypop.com
"Search 59,000 news sites, weblogs and RSS feeds for current events
and breaking news."

Eatonweb Portal
http://portal.eatonweb.com
A huge list of blogs.

Forbes Best Blog Guide
www.forbes.com/personaltech2003/04/14/bestblogslander.html
This list should help you wade through the ever-rising tide of blog
sludge.

FourOnTour
http://geocities.com/fourontour
There are thousands of travel blogs out there, and many of them are
profoundly dull. This is one of the better ones: it follows the adventures of four Brits making their way around the globe.

Going Underground
http://london-underground.blogspot.com
Adventures below the streets of London.

KICK-AAS
http://kickaas.typepad.com
"Kick All Agricultural Subsidies" is a brilliant blog devoted to third world issues

Librarian.net
www.librarian.net
A model blog, with a crucial insight into the subterranean world of the librarian.

The Londonist
www.londonist.com
Award-winning blog covering all sorts of stuff, from news and reviews to cinema and culture. The site is well laid out and funny.

MetaFilter
www.metafilter.com
Long-standing community weblog.

nyclondon
www.nyclondon.com/blog
Stunning photoblog.

Pixelsurgeon
www. pixelsurgeon.com
Easy-to-navigate blog of oddities and observations from and of the World Wide Web. As well as the regular posts, there are interviews, features and reviews, and lots of lovely pictures too.

Pop Culture Junk Mail
www.popculturejunkmail.com
Your guide to the flotsam of post-industrial society.

PubSub
www.pubsub.com
Subscribe to this service, enter a few keywords and PubSub will let you know when there are new blog posts that match your interests.

Shiny Shiny
http://shinyshiny.tv
What the world has been waiting for – a girls' guide to gadgets.

Talking Points Memo
www.talkingpointsmemo.com
All the dirt from the Washington DC Beltway.

Vagabonding
www.vagabonding.com
Great travel blog by Mike Pugh.

Books & Literature

If a squillion Web pages aren't enough to satisfy your lust for the written word, maybe you should use one to order a book. You'll be spoilt for choice, with hundreds of shops offering millions of titles for delivery worldwide. That includes many Web-only superstores such as **Amazon** as well as most of the major high-street chains (many of which operate their sites "in partnership" with **Amazon** or another online retailer). These superstores typically lay on all the trimmings: user ratings, reviews, recommendations, sample chapters, author interviews, bestseller lists, press clippings, publishing news, secure ordering and gift-wrapping. They also generally offer serious reductions, though these are usually offset by shipping costs. The UK big boys are:

Amazon www.amazon.co.uk
Blackwell's http://blackwell.com
BOL www.uk.bol.com
Bookzone www.bookzone.co.uk
Country Books www.countrybookshop.co.uk
Tesco www.tesco.com/books
Waterstone's www.waterstones.co.uk
WHSmith www.bookshop.co.uk

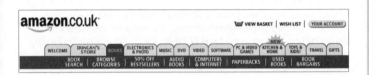

You can search across many stores simultaneously for availability and the best price by going to:

AddAll www.addall.com
BookBrain www.bookbrain.co.uk
Kelkoo http://uk.kelkoo.com

Can't find it online? Why not try searching by specialism in the **BookSellers.org** directories for UK listings...

BookSellers www.booksellers.org.uk

Or worldwide...

BookWeb.org www.bookweb.org/bookstores

books & literature

Alternatively, browse the following selection of the best book and literature sites...

Audiobook Collection
www.audiobookcollection.com
Thousands of audiobook titles for sale. A larger selection can be found at the American sites, Talking Book World and Audible:
www.talkingbooks.com
www.audible.com

Banned Books Online
http://onlinebooks.library.upenn.edu/banned-books.html
Extracts from books that riled the righteous.

Bartleby
www.bartleby.com
Online versions of such classic reference texts as Gray's *Anatomy*, Strunk & White's *The Elements of Style*, the King James Bible and works of fiction and verse by H.G. Wells, Emily Dickinson and many others.

Bibliomania
www.bibliomania.com
Houses the digital versions of some eight hundred classic literary works. However, Bibliomania also features study aids as well as digital versions of reference books, plus a shopping facility if you'd prefer the real thing.

Bodleian Library
www.bodley.ox.ac.uk
The homepage of Oxford's university library houses such digital library projects as the Broadside Ballads Project, the Internet Library of Early Journals, Allegro Catalogues of Japanese and Chinese books, the Toyota City Imaging project plus an array of images from medieval texts.

Book-A-Minute
www.rinkworks.com/bookaminute
Knock over the classics in a lunch hour.

BookCloseouts
www.bookcloseouts.com
Millions of books slightly past their shelf life.

Book Crossing
www.bookcrossing.com
Print out a unique ID label, stick it on your finished-with book and then leave it on a train or park bench. If someone finds it and likes it, they'll follow the instructions on the label, go to the site, leave a message and review and then "release" it again. Some books have now changed hands more than twenty times.

The Bookseller
www.thebookseller.com
UK book trade news, bestseller lists and more. For US publishing news, complete with author road schedules and content from *Publisher's Weekly* and *Library Journal*, see:
www.bookwire.com

The British Library
www.bl.uk
The British Library's site is more use to academics and researchers than to most ordinary Joes, but bookworms will delight in the ability to search the entire catalogue online as well as view select exhibits from the library's collection. There are also some beautifully present-ed, fully interactive versions of classic texts, complete with turning pages and a magnifying glass:
www.bl.uk/collections/treasures/digitisation4.html

Carol Hurst's Children's Literature Site
www.carolhurst.com
Reviews of books for kids, as well as ideas on how to incorporate them into the curriculum.

Classic Novels – In Five Minutes a Day
www.classic-novels.com
Get masterworks such as *Oliver Twist* or *Huckleberry Finn* emailed to you in free bite-sized instalments.

books & literature

The Electronic Labyrinth
http://eserver.org/elab
An exploration of the implications that the hyperlink has for the future of literature.

The Electronic Text Center
http://etext.lib.virginia.edu
The University of Virginia's digital archive project is similar to the others but it includes more foreign language texts than any of the competition, so if you're after esoterica like Mescalero Apache texts or just Voltaire's *Candide* in the original French, this is the place to look.

E Server
www.eserver.org
Over 30,000 online works, including classic novels, academic articles, journals, recipes and plays.

Fray
www.fray.com
A beautifully presented site of regularly updated short stories.

Gallery of "Misused" Quotation Marks
www.juvalamu.com/qmarks
A proofreader's revenge on the world. Not to be confused with the Apostrophe Protection Society:
www.apostrophe.fsnet.co.uk

The Internet Public Library
www.ipl.org
Browse online books, magazines, journals and newspapers.

January Magazine
www.januarymagazine.com
Dissecting books and authors.

Journal Storage
www.jstor.org
Organization devoted to digitally archiving scholarly journals.

JournalismNet
www.journalismnet.com
Tips and tools for tapping into the big cheat sheet. More facts for hacks at:
www.facsnet.org
www.usus.org

Literary Marketplace
www.literarymarketplace.com
Find publishers and literary agents to pester with your manuscript.

London Review of Books
www.lrb.co.uk
Everything you'd expect from the paper version of this literary institution, including a good – if not complete – archive of articles from writers such as Christopher Hitchens, Iain Sinclair, Edward Said and Marjorie Garber. See also *The New York Review of Books*:
www.nybooks.com

MysteryNet
www.mysterynet.com
Hmm, now what could this be?

Online Book Pages
http://onlinebooks.library.upenn.edu
Searches and links to around 20,000 free online books.

Perseus Digital Library
www.perseus.tufts.edu
Hundreds of translated Greek and Roman classics. For more ancient and medieval literature, see also:
http://sunsite.berkeley.edu/OMACL

Poetry.com
www.poetry.com
Your complete poetry resource, featuring literally millions of poets, plus advice on rhyming and technique, online poetry slams, the hundred greatest poems and love poems. If you're good enough, they'll even publish your own.

books & literature

eBooks

As if the Internet hadn't already sparked enough publishing, along comes the electronic book or eBook. At the moment, most eBooks are simply regular books converted into a special eBook format – or plain old Acrobat .pdf format – so you can read them either on a computer, a pocket PC, a palmtop or a dedicated eBook device.

Once you have the necessary software:

Adobe www.adobe.com/products/ebookreader
Microsoft www.microsoft.com/reader

You can choose titles from a specialist eBookshop:

eBooks www.ebooks.com
GemStar www.gemstar-ebook.com
PeanutPress www.PeanutPress.com

Or from someone offering free eBooks:

Blackmask www.blackmask.com
Free eBooks www.free-ebooks.net

Or from the eBook departments of the major book retailers:

Amazon www.amazon.co.uk/ebooks
Barnes & Noble http://ebooks.barnesandnoble.com

For news, reviews and info on eBook hardware and software, visit:

Planet eBook www.planetebook.com
eBook Web www.ebookweb.org

Or to try and get your own eBook published, go to:

Authors Online www.authorsonline.co.uk
Online Originals www.onlineoriginals.com
Mushroom eBooks www.mushroom-ebooks.com

Poetry Society
www.poetrysociety.org.uk
A halfway house for budding poets and their victims. Give it a go
– you won't be the worst in the class. Also rhyme your way to:
www.poets.org

PowerPoint Hamlet
www.myrtle.co.uk/art/hamlet
The Bard's greatest work as a PowerPoint presentation. And if you
fancy reading the Sonnets on your iPod, or the plays as PDFs, visit:
www.westering.com/ipod
www.hn.psu.edu/faculty/jmanis/shake.htm

Project Gutenberg
www.gutenberg.net
Copyrights don't live for ever; they eventually expire. In the US, that's
seventy-five years after first publication. In Europe, it's some seventy
years after the author's death. With this in mind, Project Gutenberg
is gradually bringing thousands of old texts online, along with some
more recent donations. See also:
http://digital.library.upenn.edu/books

Random Access Memory
http://randomaccessmemory.org
A truly wonderful concept: this vast repository of memories (of anything at all) is the embodiment of what the Web is meant to be all
about. Simple, compelling, about real people and real lives, with no
corporate intrusion.

Religious and Sacred Texts
http://davidwiley.com/religion.html
Links to online versions of the holy books of many of the world's
major religions – everything from the Bhagavad Ghita to the Zand-i
Vohuman Yasht.

Science Fiction Weekly
www.scifi.com/sfw
The first portal of any worth for both Isaac Asimov and Gene
Rodenberry fans.

books & literature

Shakespeare
www.opensourceshakespeare.com
There's loads of Will's work to be found online. Also see:
http://absoluteshakespeare.com
http://shakespeare.palomar.edu

The Slot: A Spot For Copy Editors
www.theslot.com
Soothing words of outrage for grammar pedants.

Text files
www.textfiles.com
Chunks of the junk that orbited the pre-Web Internet. For a slightly more modern slant, see:
www.etext.org

Urban Legends
www.urbanlegends.com
Separate the amazing-but-true from the popular myths. And when you are done here, try:
www.snopes.com

Vatican Library
www.vatican.va/library_archives/vat_library
A beautiful website heaving with beautiful religious book type stuff.

Village Voice Literary Supplement
www.villagevoice.com/vls
The online version of *The Village Voice*'s literary supplement is the complete printed version for non-New York residents and includes writing from major new voices and insightful reviews.

Web Del Sol
http://webdelsol.com
A portal for small literary reviews and journals, hosting such prestigious American names as *Kenyon Review*, *Mudlark*, *Sulfur* and *Prairie Schooner*.

Word Counter
www.wordcounter.com
Paste in your composition to rank your most overused words.

The Word Detective
www.word-detective.com
Words never escape him. See also:
www.quinion.com/words

Yournovel.com
www.yournovel.com
Star in your very own romantic novel...

Business

These homepages of prominent business magazines offer much of the same content as their paper versions, but often at a cost:

Advertising Age www.adage.com
Adweek www.adweek.com
Barrons www.barrons.com
Fast Company www.fastcompany.com
Financial Times www.ft.com
Forbes www.forbes.com
Wall Street Journal www.wsj.com

business

See also News, Newspapers and Magazines (p.197) and Money and Banking (p.162). Or browse a few of these worthy sites:

AccountingWeb
www.accountingweb.co.uk
Safe playpen for British beancounters.

Adbusters
www.adbusters.org
Headquarters of the world's culture jammers, dedicated to declaring independence from the ever-encroaching corporate state. More culture jamming to be found at ®TMArk and Blow the Dot Out Your Ass:
www.rtmark.com
www.blowthedotoutyourass.com

Ad Critic
www.adcritic.com
Make a cuppa while you wait for this year's best US TV ads. For the best of the past twenty, see:
www.usatvads.com

Ad Forum
www.adforum.com
Gateway to thousands of agencies, their ads and the humble creatives behind them. Also visit:
www.sourcetv.com

Setting up shop online

Check out the services offered by these sites:

FreeMerchant www.freemerchant.com
BigStep www.bigstep.com
BizFinity www.bizfinity.com
JumboStore www.jumbostore.com
Click and Build www.clickandbuild.com
Yahoo! http://store.yahoo.com

Or to set up an online shop for next to nothing try one of the big names, such as **eBay** or **Amazon**; alternatively turn to **Cafepress** and its growing network of over two million people:

Cafepress www.cafepress.com

Once things take off you'll need to worry about accepting credit card payments; there are now several recognized online payment methods which are worth investigating; read the FAQs of these sites:

Worldpay www.worldpay.com
BidPay www.bidpay.com
PayPal www.paypal.com

Annual Report Gallery
www.reportgallery.com
View the annual reports of over two thousand publicly traded companies for free.

Bizymoms
www.bizymoms.com
Crafty ways to cash up without missing the afternoon soaps.

Business.com
www.business.com
Attempting to become the Yahoo! of business sites.

Business Advice Online
www.businessadviceonline.org.uk
Information and advice on taxes, regulations, e-commerce and con-

business

sultations from the Small Business Service. For more resources see:
www.businesslink.org

Business Ethics
www.business-ethics.com
Apparently it's not an oxymoron.

BVCA
www.bvca.co.uk
Homepage of the British Venture Capital Association, offering basic advice for businesses seeking funding.

City Wire
www.citywire.co.uk
Probably the best place to come for UK financial news. City Wire also contains research reports on what the directors are up to.

Clickz
www.clickz.com
The Web as seen by the marketing biz.

Cluetrain Manifesto
www.cluetrain.org
Modern-day translation of "the customer is always right". Read it or perish. Alternatively, if you'd prefer an update on "never give a sucker an even break", consult the Ferengi Rules of Acquisition:
www.dmwright.com/html/ferengi.htm

Confederation of British Industry
www.cbi.org.uk/home.html
Tomorrow's public policy today.

Customers Suck!
www.customerssuck.com
Grumbling dispatches from the retail front.

Delphion Intellectual Property Network
www.delphion.com
Sift through a few decades of international patents plus a gallery of obscurities. Ask the right questions and you might stumble across tomorrow's technology long before the media. For UK patents see: www.patent.gov.uk

DTI
www.dti.gov.uk
The homepage of the Department for Trade and Industry offers policy news and resources that affect every UK business.

Entrepreneur.com
www.entrepreneur.com
"Get rich now, ask us how."

Flame Broiled
www.geocities.com/capitolhill/lobby/2645
The disgruntled ex-Burger King employee homepage. If only every company had one.

Flounder's Mission Statement Generator
www.giantflounderpenis.com/mission.html
It is this site's "business to holistically re-engineer economically sound resources to exceed customer expectations".

The Foundation Center
http://fdncenter.org
Companies who might happily spare you a fiver.

Garage.com
www.garage.com
Matchmaking agency for entrepreneurs and investors founded by Apple's Guy Kawasaki. For more, see: www.moneyhunter.com

business

Guerrilla Marketing
www.gmarketing.com
Get ahead by metaphorically butchering your competitors' families
and poisoning your customers' water supply.

Inc
www.inc.com
Online presence of American mag for entrepreneurs and small businesses; includes advice and services such as assistance with creating
marketing plans, health insurance quotes and financing.

InfoUSA
www.infousa.com
Find likely Americans to bug with your presentation.

International Trademark Association
http://inta.org
Protect your brand identity.

Internal Memos
www.internalmemos.com
Leaked.

Mondaq
www.mondaq.com
Regulatory information and financial commentary on over eighty
world economies.

Nitro Marketing Mindset
www.nitromindset.com
How to murder brain-dead Web surfers with HTML.

Patent Café
www.patentcafe.com
Protect your crackpot schemes and see them through to fruition.

Planet Feedback
www.planetfeedback.com
Let US companies know what you think of their service.

Disgruntled customer sites

The Web may be the most important business tool ever invented, but it just may be the most important consumer tool ever invented as well. This is what happens when companies don't follow the "customer is always right" rule, or just get too big for their boots.

BT Open Woe www.btopenwoe.co.uk
Ford Really Sucks www.fordreallysucks.com
Fuck Microsoft www.fuckmicrosoft.com
Fuck McDonalds www.fuckmcdonalds.co.uk

And if you want to tell the corporate scum how you feel, first take a moment to search **Google** for "complaint letter of the year" for a little inspiration.

The Prince's Trust
www.princes-trust.org.uk
Learn new skills thanks to Charlie.

Statistical Data Locators
www.ntu.edu.sg/library/stat/statdata.htm
This site contains links to the economic and demographic data of just about every world economy.

Super Marketing: Ads from the Comic Books
www.steveconley.com/supermarketing.htm
The ads that kept you lying awake at night wishing you had more money.

The Wonderful Wankometer
www.cynicalbastards.com/wankometer
Measure corporate hyperbole. Couple with:
www.dack.com/web/bullshit.html

Cars & Motor Bikes

Before you're sharked into signing for a new or used vehicle, go online and check out a few road tests and price guides. You can complete the entire exercise while you're there, but it mightn't hurt to drive one first. Start here:

Autobytel www.autobytel.com
Autolocate www.autolocate.co.uk
Autotrader www.autotrader.co.uk
BBC Top Gear www.topgear.beeb.com
Car Importing www.carimporting.co.uk
Car Shop www.carshop.co.uk
Carseekers www.carseekers.co.uk
DealerNet www.dealernet.com
Exchange & Mart www.exchangeandmart.co.uk
4 Car www.4car.co.uk
Kelly Blue Book www.kbb.com
Oneswoop www.oneswoop.com
Upgrade Your Car www.upgradeyourcar.com
What Car? www.whatcar.com

WHATCAR? For expert, impartial advice

Automobile Association
www.theaa.com
Not merely an online rest stop trying to hawk you memberships, the AA's site has useful free features such as a cheap petrol finder and route planner. See also the RAC or International Breakdown:
www.rac.co.uk
www.internationalbreakdown.com

Bike Trader
www.biketrader.co.uk
Part of the Autotrader group, this site offers the same services as its parent site: good search tool, advice on buying and selling motor bikes, and links to insurance and finance companies.

Breath Testing
www.copsonline.com/breath_test.htm
Slurring your swearwords, wobbling all over the road, mounting gutters and knocking kids off bikes? Pull over and blow into this site.

Car Net
www.carnet.co.uk
Massive automotive portal, including advice and information on collecting, research facilities, trivia, forums, links, classifieds, want ads, rallying news and more.

Circuit Driver
www.circuitdriver.com
This e-zine for speed junkies includes racing information (with online booking facilities), car reviews, etc.

Classic Car Directory
www.classic-car-directory.com
Good resource for classic car enthusiasts, with price guides, dealer directories, events listings, classifieds and links.

The Highway Code
www.highwaycode.gov.uk
Fail your driving theory test online first.

Lowrider.com
www.lowrider.com
Online community for Vatos Locos and other connoisseurs of barely-street-legal motor vehicles with the lowest clearance known to man.

MOT
www.ukmot.com
Let Malcolm the mechanic help you make your car roadworthy.

cars & motor bikes

Motorcycle News
www.motorcyclenews.com
Everything on two wheels ... plus the obligatory bikini babes. Also
see BikersWeb and, for a more measured approach, the Motorcycle
Action Group:
www.bikersweb.co.uk
www.mag-uk.org

Parkers Online
www.parkers.co.uk
Car price and specs database going back
twenty years. For new models, try:
www.new-car-net.co.uk

Planet Campers
www.planetcampers.com
The online home of all things VW-camper-related – loads of ads,
links for buying and selling and useful books. Also see:
www.vwcampers.co.uk

Speedtraps
www.ukspeedtraps.co.uk
A great resource for drivers who want to know, umm, where traffic
flashpoints might occur.

Street Trucks Magazine
www.streettrucksmag.com
Custom trucking bible for fans of bags, grilles, rims, souped-up air
intake manifolds and other such things.

Woman Motorist
www.womanmotorist.com
The demographic group that motor vehicle insurers prefer. For the best deals, try:
www.diamond.co.uk

World Parts
www.world-parts.com
If you're seeking a hubcap or an entire engine, tell this site the car's make and model and the country in which you live, and it will tell you who stocks your part. Also try Find a Part:
www.find-a-part.com

Classifieds

Online classifieds need no explanation. They're like the paper version, but easier to search and possibly more up to date. In fact, most papers are moving their classifieds to the Net, though you might have to pay to see the latest listings. Here's a small selection:

Ad-Mart www.ad-mart.co.uk
Ad Trader www.adtrader.co.uk
Exchange & Mart www.exchangeandmart.co.uk
Excite Classifieds http://classifieds.excite.com
Friday-Ad www.friday-ad.co.uk
London Classifieds www.londonclassified.com
Loot www.loot.com
Net Trader www.nettrader.co.uk
Photo Ads www.photoads.co.uk
Preloved www.preloved.co.uk
Reel Exchange www.reelexchange.co.uk
Sell It Net www.sellitnet.com

Computing & Tech News

Every decent PC brand has a site where you can download the latest drivers, get support and find out what's new. It won't be hard to find. Usually it's the company name or initials between a www and a com.

So you'll find **Dell** at www.dell.com, **Compaq** at www.compaq.com, **Gateway** at www.gateway.com, and so forth. Most of the big names also have international branches, which will be linked from the main site. Consult **Yahoo!** if that fails. If you're in the market for new computer bits, check out the best price across online vendors:

AnandTech www.anandtech.com/guides
Price Watch www.pricewatch.com
StreetPrices.com http://Europe.StreetPrices.com

Popular package software vendors include:

Buy.com www.buy.com
Chumbo.com www.chumbo.com
Jungle.com www.jungle.com

Bear in mind that if you buy from US sites, imports might be taxed upon arrival. It's worth browsing a few of the online mags for reviews before you buy; try:

Maxpc www.maxpc.co.uk
PC Answers www.pcanswers.co.uk
PCWorld www.pcworld.com
Personal Computer World www.pcw.co.uk

Here are a few more of our favourite tech sites:

Bastard Operator from Hell
http://bofh.ntk.net
If you work in a big office, you know this man.

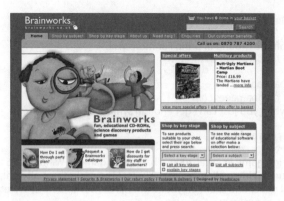

Brainworks
www.brainworks.co.uk
A great site where you can stock up with software for the little ones.

Chankstore FreeFont Archive
www.chank.com/freefonts.htm
Download a wacky Chank Diesel display font free each week. If there's still space in your font sack, arrive hat in hand at:
www.printerideas.com/fontfairy
www.pizzadude.dk/fonts.php
www.fontface.com
www.flashkit.com/fonts

Clip Art
http://webclipart.about.com
Bottomless cesspit of the soulless dross used to inject life into documents. Also click through to:
http://classroomclipart.com

CNET
www.cnet.com
Daily technology news and features plus reviews, shopping, games and downloads, along with schedules, transcripts and related stories from CNET's broadcasting network.

computing & tech news

Desktop Publishing
http://desktoppublishing.com
Get off the ground in print. For more visit:
http://desktoppub.about.com

Dingbat Pages
www.dingbatpages.com
For when you just can't get enough symbol fonts.

Easter egg archive
www.eeggs.com
A racing game in Excel 2000, a basketball game in Windows 95 and a raygun-wielding alien in Quark Xpress? They're in there all right, but you'll never find them on your own. Here's how to unlock secrets in scores of programs.

Electronic Privacy Information Center
www.epic.org
Since 1994, EPIC has been in the vanguard of the campaign to protect privacy over the Internet. For a withering attack on the UK's Regulation of Investigatory Powers Act and coverage of free speech issues on the Net, go to:
www.fipr.org
www.eff.org

Forward Garden
www.forwardgarden.com
The resting place of every piece of junk email you've ever received. True masochists should also tune their browser into:
www.spamradio.org

Ghost Sites: The Museum of Failure
www.disobey.com/ghostsites
A chronicle of the rise and fall of the cyber empire.

Gibson Research Corporation
http://grc.com
If you're at all interested in computer security or are a raving paranoiac, you owe it to yourself to check out this site.

Apple online

Apple www.apple.com

The company's own site is the essential drop-in to update your Mac, pick up QuickTime and be hard-sold the latest hardware. To top up with news, software, and brand affirmations, see:

MacAddict www.macaddict.com
Apple Insider www.appleinsider.com
Tidbits www.tidbits.com
Mac In Touch www.macintouch.com
MacNN www.macnn.com
MacSlash www.macslash.com

And if you want to know what Apple is going to come out with next, angle your one-button mouse at:

Mac Rumors www.macrumors.com

For the latest applications, hints and news on OS X Tiger, seek out:

Mac OS X Apps www.macosxapps.com
Mac OS X Hints www.macosxhints.com

If you're still desperately clinging on to your old Quadra or Performa, try:

Low End Mac www.lowendmac.com

And to diagnose your ailing Mac:

MacFixit www.macfixit.com

And if iPods are what float your boat, take a trip to one of these sites:

Apple/iPod www.apple.com/ipod
iPodLounge www.ipodlounge.com

Alternatively, pick up a copy of *The Rough Guide to iPods, iTunes & Music Online*. And while you're at it, we also recommend *The Rough Guide to Macs & OS X*.

The GNU Project
www.gnu.org
The homepage of Richard Stallman's efforts to create a free operating system. You might know it better as Linux, named after Linus Torvald's kernel. For more on GNU/Linux, try:
www.linux.org

Guide to Flaming
www.advicemeant.com/flame
Learn how to win friends and influence people in newsgroups, forums and chat rooms.

Hackers' Homepage
www.hackershomepage.com
Everything you shouldn't do to your computer or someone else's. Just make sure you run every antivirus utility you've got after stopping by. More at:
www.attrition.org
www.cultdeadcow.com
www.2600.com

InfoAnarchy
www.infoanarchy.org
Turn to this site for all the latest news and views from the battle to keep information free.

Internet Speed Test
www.zensupport.co.uk/speedtest
Wallow in the grim truth about the speed of your connection. More tests to be found at:
www.dslreports.com/stest
www.beelinebandwidthtest.com

ISP Review
www.ispreview.co.uk
Compare your Internet Service Provider with the rest and get the latest broadband news. Also try:
www.net4nowt.com
www.broadband-help.com/home.asp

Online storage

Whether you want to back-up some files safely onto a remote server or transfer large amounts of data between two computers, consider signing up for some online storage. Some webspace may have come free with your Internet access account (ask your ISP). If it did, all you'll need is an FTP client to upload and download files to the space. Such as:

CuteFTP www.cuteftp.com

If it didn't, you could find some free space from:

FreeWebspace www.freewebspace.net

Alternatively, if you don't mind paying, sign up for a virtual disk drive service, such as:

XDrive www.xdrive.com
.Mac www.mac.com

IT Reviews

www.itreviews.co.uk
Independent, jargon-free reviews of hardware, software, games, etc. For more reviews, try these:
http://compreviews.about.com/compute/compreview
www.technologyowl.com

Microsoft

www.microsoft.com
If you're running any Microsoft product (and the chance of that seems to be approaching 100 percent), drop by this disorganized scrapheap regularly for upgrades, news, support and patches. That includes the latest free tweaks to Windows, Office and all that falls under the Internet Explorer regime.

Modem Help

www.modemhelp.org
Solve your dial-up dramas for modems of all persuasions including cable, ISDN and DSL. And be sure to check your modem maker's page for driver and firmware upgrades.

computing & tech news

The Museum of Counter Art
www.counterart.com
"THE showcase for over 500 sets of counter digit artwork."

Need to Know
www.ntk.net
Weekly high-tech wrap-up with a sarcastic bite.

Newslinx
www.newslinx.com
Have the top Net technology stories, aggregated from around fifty sources, delivered to your mailbox daily.

Old Computers
www.old-computers.com
Relive the days when your Sinclair ZX81 or Commodore Vic 20 could barely play solitaire. More at HCM:
www.homecomputer.de

Old English Computer Glossary
www.u.arizona.edu/~ctb/wordhord.html
All your favourite computer terms translated into Arthurian dialect.

Palmgear
www.palmgear.com
Know your Palm like the back of your hand. For the PocketPC, see:
www.pocketmatrix.com

PC Mechanic
www.pcmech.com/byopc
How to build or upgrade your own computer. Also see:
http://arstechnica.com/tweak/hardware.html

PC Tweaking
www.anandtech.com
How to overclock your processor into the next millennium, tweak
your bios and upgrade your storage capacity to attract members of
the opposite sex. Loads more at:
www.arstechnica.com
www.geek.com
www.pcextremist.com
www.sharkyextreme.com
www.shacknews.com
www.tweaktown.com

PCWebopedia
www.pcwebopedia.com
Superb illustrated encyclopedia of computer technology.

computing & tech news

PC help

The best place to find an answer to your computer problems is usually on Usenet. Chances are it's already been answered, so before you rush in and post, search the archives through Google Groups.

Google Groups http://groups.google.com

That's not to say you won't find an answer on the Web. You probably will, so follow up with a Web search. You'll find a choice of engines at the very bottom of the results page. If you click on **Google**, for example, it will perform the same search in the Web database. Apart from Usenet, there are several very active computing forums on the Web, such as:

Computing.net www.computing.net
Tek-Tips www.tek-tips.com

And there are hundreds of troubleshooting and Windows news sites, such as:

ActiveWin www.activewin.com
Annoyances.org www.annoyances.org
Virtual Dr http://virtualdr.com
WinosCentral www.winoscentral.com

Don't forget to keep your hardware installation drivers up to date. You'll find the latest files for download direct from the manufacturer's website, or at driver guides such as these:

DriverForum www.driverforum.com
Driver Guide www.driverguide.com
Drivers HQ www.drivershq.com
WinDrivers.com www.windrivers.com

The Register
www.theregister.co.uk
Punchy tech news that spins to its own tune.

SafeWeb
www.safeweb.com
Originally designed for surfers in countries with repressive regimes, SafeWeb is a service that encrypts all data sent from and received by your computer while surfing the Net so that all of your downloads

are safe from those prying eyes. For more anonymous surfing, try
The Anonymizer:
www.anonymizer.com

Scantips
www.scantips.com
Become a scan-do type of dude.

Slashdot.org
http://slashdot.org
News for those who've entirely given up on the human race.

Tech Dirt
www.techdirt.com
Keeping tabs on the dark
underbelly of the Internet
economy.

Techtales
www.techtales.com
Customers – they might
always be right but they
sure do ask the darnedest
things.

Tom's Hardware Guide
www.tomshardware.com
One of the most important sites on the Net, at least for the hardware industry. Tom and his reporters are credited with the delayed
release of Pentium's 1GHz Pentium III processor because the site
gave it a thumbs down. This is the best source for bug reports and
benchmark tests.

WebReference
www.webreference.com
If you don't know your HTML from your XML or DHTML, try this reference and tutorials site. For more tips and tricks, try Webmonkey:
http://webmonkey.wired.com/webmonkey

computing & tech news

Wired News
www.wired.com
The Net's best source of breaking technology news plus archives of *Wired* magazine. For more, try Geek.com:
www.geek.com

Woody's Office Portal
www.wopr.com
Beat some sense out of Microsoft Office. For Outlook, see:
www.slipstick.com/outlook

Computer viruses

Unless you're 100 percent certain that a download or attachment is safe, even if it's been sent by your best friend, DON'T OPEN IT! Instead, save it to your Desktop or a quarantine folder and examine it carefully before proceeding. That should include running it past an up-to-date antivirus scanner such as AVG (www.grisoft.com). You'll find everything you need to know about viruses at:

About http://antivirus.about.com
Faqs.org www.faqs.org/faqs/computer-virus
Grisoft www.grisoft.com
Symantec www.symantec.com/avcenter

Yahoo! Computing
www.yahoo.com/Computers
The grandpappy of all computing directories.

ZDNet
www.zdnet.com
Computing info powerhouse from Ziff Davis, publisher of *PC Magazine*, *MacUser*, *Computer Gaming World* and scores of other IT titles. Each magazine donates content such as news, product reviews and lab test results; plus there's a ton of prime Net-exclusive technochow. The best place to start researching anything even vaguely computer-related.

Crafts

About Hobbies
www.about.com/hobbies
Your first portal of call for any crafts search should be About's
impressive hobbies page which contains links to their basketry,
beadwork, candle-making and woodworking sites as well as twenty
other crafts sites that they host.

Classic Stitches
www.classicstitches.com
The homepage of *Classic Stitches* magazine includes some 150
downloadable charts to set your needles working.

Crafts Council
www.craftscouncil.org.uk
News on and listings of craft shows, events, exhibitions, seminars
and workshops. The Crafts Council also provides a regional list of
shops selling contemporary crafts as well as buying guides.

Crafts Unlimited
www.crafts-unlimited.co.uk
Over 1100 cross-stitch patterns to buy, plus downloadable beginner's and advanced guides to cross-stitch technique. Also check out
Cross-Stitch Design:
www.maurer-stroh.com

Home Sewing Association
www.sewing.org
An essential bookmark for budding Gallianos and hopeless bach-
elors alike. The site is packed with sewing lessons for beginners and
tips and trends and advanced techniques for more experienced
seamstresses.

Internet Craft Fair
www.craft-fair.co.uk
Put a stitch in time at this massive online community for the UK's
crafts scene.

Planet Patchwork
www.planetpatchwork.com
Blocks and vectors of info devoted to the mystique of quilting.

Wool Works
www.woolworks.org
Containing an archive of more than 250 patterns, an extensive hints and tips section on making socks and knitting for dolls, and a comprehensive links page – this is a darn good knitting site.

Education

This chapter is perhaps a bit of a misnomer as the entire Internet is potentially the greatest single educational resource that's ever been invented: the latter-day equivalent of the library at Alexandria. Here you'll find educational resources (for students, teachers and parents), general homework sites, information on distance learning and admissions guides. For other study tools, try the Reference chapter or other subject headings (Art, Politics, History, etc.).

About Education
http://education.about.com
They may be geared towards the US, but, as usual, About's education pages are an excellent source of information and news. Having trouble with times tables or conjugating Latin verbs? Try About Homework:
http://homework.about.com

Academic Info
www.academicinfo.net
Research directory for students and teachers.

Ask an Expert
www.cln.org/int_expert.html
Links to hundreds of experts who will happily answer your homework question or offer you careers advice. There are also teaching experts awaiting questions from harried pedagogues.

Best websites for Students

www.unn.ac.uk/~iniw2/bestsite.htm

Links to help you write your next essay.

Channel 4: Homework High

www.homeworkhigh.co.uk

Channel 4's homework site allows you to ask experts questions and browse the archive of responses. Much better than the BBC's similar site because it's not linked to the station's programmes.

Click Teaching

www.clickteaching.com

Primary school teachers' site largely written by primary teachers.

EduFind

www.edufind.com

Massive education resource site, with a TEFL slant.

Evil House of Cheat

www.cheathouse.com

Thousands of college essays, term papers and reports. But beware, teachers can check for traces of plagiarism:

www.turnitin.com

Good Schools Guide

www.goodschoolsguide.co.uk

Unfortunately, in order to gain full access to this very useful site, you need to buy the paper version of the popular book, which then lets you get to the weekly updates and the school reviews written by parents for parents.

Guide to Grammar and Style

http://andromeda.rutgers.edu/~jlynch/Writing

Handy online guide to English language usage. It won't replace Strunk & White or *The Chicago Manual of Style*, but if you're in a pinch, could be worth a try.

education

International Centre for Distance Learning
http://www-icdl.open.ac.uk
The Open University's distance learning resource centre contains a huge database on courses and organizations as well as abstracts of journal articles and research papers pertaining to distance education.

Internet Public Library
www.ipl.org
Browse the catalogue of some 16,000 online texts, utilize the original resources and ask homework questions – all without a horn-rimmed librarian telling you to down your Discman.

ISIS
www.isis.org.uk
The homepage of the Independent Schools Information Service allows parents and teachers to search their database for information on prospective schools and employers.

Learn.co.uk
www.learn.co.uk
A huge resource for both students and teachers, with dowloadable sample SATs, lesson plans, an online community for teachers, revision advice and information on the national curriculum.

Learning Alive
www.learningalive.co.uk
It claims to be the largest educational resource on the Net, but to access its Living Library (where most of these resources are stored), you have to subscribe – at £50 a year.

Maths Net
www.mathsnet.net
For help with numbers.

National Curriculum Online
www.nc.uk.net
The Government's definitive national curriculum site for teachers. For the Scottish curriculum, go to the Scottish CCC Homepage: www.sccc.ac.uk

National Grid for Learning

www.ngfl.gov.uk

This site is the centrepiece of the Government's plans to harness the Net as the future of education. As you might guess, it's a bit of a sprawling mess, but there are sections devoted to just about every educational issue you can think of, as well as tons of links, a virtual teacher centre and so on.

National Union of Students

www.nus.org.uk

How to buy a pint if your grant runs out.

Profquotes

www.profquotes.com

They sure do say the darnedest things.

SearchEdu

www.searchedu.com

Search millions of university and education pages.

Study Abroad

www.studyabroad.com

Hop to grass that's greener.

StudyWeb

www.studyweb.com

An absolutely enormous education portal, with links to some 160,000 resources, all organized by grade level (some translation from American English required).

education

The Teacher Network
www.theteachernet.co.uk
Resources, links, job search for teachers.

Thesis
www.thesis.com
Online version of the *Times Higher Education Supplement*.

Topmarks Education
www.topmarks.co.uk
This excellent and very easy-to-use site searches the Web for educational sites pertaining to your subject and appropriate age level, so if you're searching for sites to help you with GCSE revision it will weed out all the sites aimed at Key Stage 1 students. See also Schoolzone: www.schoolzone.co.uk

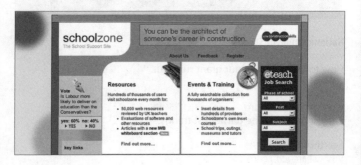

UCAS
www.ucas.co.uk
Information on university courses, including admissions requirements and general facts and figures, from the University and Colleges Admissions Service.

Unofficial Guides
www.unofficial-guides.com
Get the real dope on the unis from the students themselves, not the marketing boards.

Up My Street
www.upmystreet.com
Type in your postcode and get quick access to the performance tables of local schools.

Word Central
www.wordcentral.com
A site designed to broaden kids' vocabulary by introducing them to the joys of wordplay. There's also a section for teachers with lesson plans and a history of the English language.

Employment

If you're looking to move on up, beware that if you post your CV online your boss could find it – embarrassing at the very least. The same situation could also arise if you leave it online once you're hired. Most job agencies have sites these days, and the better ones update at least daily, so there are far too many to attempt to list here. Bigger isn't always better, as you'll find yourself competing with more applicants. On the other hand, your prospective employer isn't likely to restrict their job search to a site that isn't well known. Whether you're looking for a job or to fill a vacancy, try:

Fish4Jobs www.fish4jobs.co.uk
Go Job Site www.jobsite.co.uk
Gradunet www.gradunet.co.uk
Guardian Jobs Unlimited http://jobs.guardian.co.uk
Job Search www.jobsearch.co.uk
Monster www.monster.co.uk
Overseas Jobs www.overseasjobs.com
People Bank www.peoplebank.com
Reed www.reed.co.uk
Stepstone www.stepstone.com
Total Jobs http://totaljobs.com

employment

All Jobs UK
http://alljobsuk.com
This recruitment portal claims to give access to every job vacancy on the Internet – all two million of 'em.

A–Z Guide to British Employment Law
www.emplaw.co.uk
Get the upper hand on your boss.

Brilliant Careers
www.channel4.com/brilliantcareers
Channel 4's employment site is a no-nonsense guide to the job market, with advice, support, vacancies and personality tests.

Buzzword Bingo
www.progress.demon.co.uk/Fun/Buzzword-Bingo.html
When your boss says something along the lines of, "proactive" or "quality management system", check it off on your card – you're a winner if you complete a row.

Cool Works
www.coolworks.com
Seasonal jobs in US resorts, national parks, camps, ranches and cruise lines.

Despair Inc.
www.demotivators.com
Take the mickey out of your boss and colleagues with a range of bitter and twisted calendars and mugs.

Expat Network
www.expatnetwork.co.uk
Subscription placement and settling service for working globetrotters.

DEMOTIVATION
SOMETIMES THE BEST SOLUTION TO MORALE PROBLEMS IS
JUST TO FIRE ALL OF THE UNHAPPY PEOPLE.

FT Career Point
http://career.ft.com/careers
Advice from the suits at the *Financial Times*.

Hungry and Homeless
www.hungryandhomeless.co.uk
No, not another site mocking yesterday's dotcom millionaires, but one that houses pictures and histories of homeless people looking for work.

Integrity Based Interviewing
www.interviewing.net
Ex-federal agents show you how to get to the truth without drawing any blood.

Internet Career Guide
www.careerguide.net
This directory functions for both jobseekers and employers. Included are links to headhunters, CV-writing services, recruitment and outplacement services.

I-resign.com
www.i-resign.com
Quit now while you're ahead.

Mindless Jobs of America
www.geocities.com/Area51/Vault/9932/mja.html
Think your job sucks?

The Riley Guide
www.rileyguide.com
Messy but massive directory of job-hunting resources.

UK Jobs Sites
www.transdata-inter.co.uk/jobs-agencies
An excellent resource for the jobseeker, this directory lists and ranks all the major British online headhunters and ranks them by number of vacancies, services, regions and industries they serve.

Working Wounded
www.workingwounded.com
Get back at your boss and your co-workers without getting fired.

Yahoo! Careers
http://careers.yahoo.com
As ever, Yahoo! is in on the act, and as ever, does it superbly. This arm, however, handles only US placements. But key "employment" as a search term or click on "international" and you'll be awash with options spanning the globe.

Environment

Envirolink Network
http://envirolink.netforchange.com
Online community for the environmentally aware, containing links to articles on sustainable energy sources and pesticides, daily news updates and a green marketplace. See also:
www.igc.org/igc/gateway/enindex.html

Environmental Defense
www.environmentaldefense.org
In-depth site of problems, issues, solutions and links.

Environmental Organization Directory
www.eco-portal.com
Find primary production and green-minded sites.

ForestWorld
www.forestworld.com
Timber tales from both sides of the bulldozer.

Friends of the Earth
www.foe.co.uk
The homepage of the environmental pressure group features information on local, national and international campaigns, and information on the issues involved.

Greenpeace
www.greenpeace.org
In addition to the charity's campaigns, the Greenpeace homepage covers genetic engineering, ocean preservation, toxic waste and the transport of nuclear materials.

Lycos Environment News
www.ens-news.com
The Web's best source for unbiased environmental news.

Rainforest Information Portal
www.rainforestweb.org
News from the frontline against deforestation. For more try:
www.rainforest-alliance.org
www.rainforest.org

SEA and SKY
www.seasky.org
Explore the deep ocean and deep space with this excellent educational resources for kids of all ages.

UK National Air Quality Information Archive
www.airquality.co.uk
Worried about chemical factories or diesel emissions? Check the air quality for your area here. To feel guilty about the amount of carbon dioxide you are responsible for, check out the Carbon Calculator:
www.clearwater.org/carbon.html

United Nations Environment Programme
www.unep.org
Visit these pages to find out how the United Nations is planning to make a difference.

Ethical living

If you're the sort of person who worries about the impact that your life has on people and environments around the world, then the Web is an invaluable source of information – and a great place to shop. Try the following sites, or for more information check out *The Rough Guide to Ethical Shopping*.

British Association for Fair Trade Shops
www.bafts.org.uk
Locate your local fair-trade shop, for ethically sourced gifts, cards, jewellery, clothes, hand-made papers, ornaments, quilts, etc.

Buy Nothing Day
www.buynothingday.co.uk
Take part in the annual celebration of non-consumerism.

Climate Care
www.climatecare.org
Offset your greenhouse-gas emissions by paying for new trees.

Clipper
www.clipperteasshop.com
More ethical hot drinks than you could shake a teaspoon at.

Ecological Footprint Quiz
www.myfootprint.org
Calculate the total area of the earth needed to support your consumption habits. Expect a major guilt trip.

Ethical Investment Research Service
www.eiris.org
Background and links on all elements of ethical finance.

Ethical Trading Initiative
www.ethicaltrade.org
Find out which UK companies have (and haven't) signed up to the ETI, a UK organization working to stamp out sweatshops.

Boycott campaign sites

At any time there are scores of consumer boycotts underway – some serious and widely observed, other silly and obscure. Following are a few campaigns sites – to be treated, of course, as only one side of the argument. For more, visit: www.ethicalconsumer.org/boycotts/boycotts.htm

Adidas www.viva.org.uk
For using kangaroo skin in its football boots.

Bacardi www.ratb.org.uk
For using Cuban imagery while allegedly plotting to have Castro overthrown.

Drugs www.huumeboikotti.org
Why you shouldn't rail about oil firms while doing a line of Charlie.

Esso www.stopesso.com
Taking aim at the "global warming villain".

Gap www.gapsucks.org
For its owners' links to the felling of old-growth American forest in the US.

George W Bush's corporate donors www.boycottbush.net
You'd be amazed who bankrolls the US's simplest-ever president.

Gillette www.boycottgillette.com
For "using spy chips" to stop Mach 3 razor-blade theft

Nestlé www.babymilkaction.org
The breast-milk issue keeps on raging, albeit less fiercely than before.

Tiger prawns www.ejfoundation.org
Read this and you'll never again order your favourite king-prawn bhuna.

Tropical timber www.foe.co.uk
Why not to purchase that mahogany sleigh bed.

Burma www.burmacampaign.org.uk
Find out which companies have links to the brutal Burmese junta. More country boycotts at:
Canada www.boycott-canada.com
China www.boycottmadeinchina.org
Israel www.bigcampaign.org
US www.krysstal.com/democracy_whyusa_boycott.html

ethical living

Fairtrade Foundation
www.fairtrade.org.uk
Find out all about the Fairtrade label – from products to principles – from the organization that administers it in the UK.

Fish Online
www.fishonline.org
Find out which fish you can eat without worrying about falling stock levels, seabed destruction and dead dolphins, turtles and seabirds.

Farmers' Markets
www.farmersmarkets.net
Explore the aims and ideas of farmers' markets and find your local.

Fairtrade Online
www.fairtradeonline.com
Fairly traded food and more – a joint Oxfam–Traidcraft project.

Forest Stewardship Council
www.fsc-uk.info
Locate wooden products certified as having been ethically sourced.

Gossypium
www.gossypium.co.uk
Nicely cut clothes in fairly traded cotton. More ethical threads at:
www.hug.co.uk
www.ptree.co.uk

Hawkshead Organic Fish
www.organicfish.com
Once you've read about the horrors of intensive fish farming, you'll want to get all your salmon from here. And for meats:
www.graigfarm.co.uk

HippyShopper
www.hippyshopper.com
Ethical consumerism blog, with a tounge-in-cheek angle.

NFU Little Red Tractor
www.littleredtractor.org.uk
Read about the NFU's Little Red Tractor logo, which claims to ensure decent standards of animal welfare. Contrast with:

OneVillage
www.onevillage.co.uk
A huge range of ethically sourced homeware.

Open Secrets
www.opensecrets.com
Discover out which companies are oiling the wheels of US politics.

Responsible Travel
www.responsibletravel.com
Buy holidays from companies screened for ethical soundness. If you're just after flights, drop in to this charitable agent:
www.northsouthtravel.co.uk

Smile
www.smile.co.uk
Brilliant online banking from the ethically right-on Co-op Bank.

Soil Association
www.soilassociation.org.uk
The UK's best-known organic certification body. The background articles are a bit one-sided, but the directory of organic suppliers (ox schemes to is unmatched. If you'd rather grow your own, head to:
www.hdra.org.uk/gyo.htm
www.redtractortruth.com

Veg Oil Motoring
www.vegoilmotoring.com
Find out how to run your car on recycled chip fat.

Events & Entertainment

Aloud
www.aloud.com
Book music, festival and event tickets online from this member of
the Which? Code of Practice. See also Ticketmaster:
www.ticketmaster.co.uk

Ananova – Going Out
www.ananova.com
Comprehensive and nationwide general entertainment listings
which you can have sent to your WAP phone.

British Arts Festivals
www.artsfestivals.co.uk
Keep tabs on the UK's highbrow festivals from Brighton to
Edinburgh on this comprehensive site.

eFestivals
www.efestivals.co.uk
If you can't get enough of playing your bongos in the mud, point
your virtual caravan to this site which contains ticket information,
line-ups, rumours and reviews of all the major music festivals.

London Theatre Guide
www.londontheatre.co.uk
This venerable site boasts not only excellent theatre listings but
regularly updated cast news and seating plans. See also What's On
Stage for regional as well as London listings:
www.whatsonstage.com

Nightclubbin' UK
www.nightclubbinuk.com
Listings and links for a large majority of Britain's clubs.

This Is London
http://www.thisislondon.co.uk
The *Evening Standard*'s site includes film, theatre, comedy and club-bing listings for the capital, as well as a visitor's guide and reviews of pubs and restaurants.

Time Out
www.timeout.com
Definitive London listings from the venerable magazine, as well as global city guides if you're planning to venture abroad.

Webflyers
www.webflyers.co.uk
Guide to clubbing in just about every corner of this green and pleasant land; also see:
www.nightclubbinuk.com

fashion & beauty

Regional listings

Most UK events sites can seem like a Big Smoke screen with all the emphasis on London. Here are a few of the many regional listings sites that attempt to redress the balance:

Bournemouth www.bournemouth.co.uk
Brighton www.whatsonguide.co.uk
Cardiff www.metroplex.co.uk/WhatsOn/cardiff
Chester www.chestercc.gov.uk/asp/events
Coventry www.cwn.org.uk/whatson
Edinburgh www.edinburghguide.com
Hampshire www.hants.gov.uk/whatson
Manchester www.manchesteronline.co.uk
Newcastle www.tyne-online.com/whatson.asp
Sheffield www.sheffnet.co.uk/events/events.asp

Fashion & Beauty

Unless it entirely erodes your reading time, the Net isn't likely to cut your guilty expenditure on glossy mags. While there's a spree of fledgling style zines and something from nearly all the big rack names, nothing compares to getting it in print. Nonetheless it will certainly supplement your vice. What you will find the Net better for is researching products, checking out brands and saving money on consumables such as cosmetics at stores such as:

Drugstore www.drugstore.com
Gloss www.gloss.com
HQ Hair www.hqhair.com (UK)
iBeauty www.ibeauty.com
Perfumania www.perfumania.com
Perfume Shop www.theperfumeshop.com (UK)
Reflect www.reflect.com

Sephora www.sephora.com
Think Natural www.thinknatural.com (UK)

Buying clothes online is tough but popular nonetheless. They're out there, if you know what you're doing, but you'll soon see why **Boo.com** failed. Label sites are sometimes interesting for new season looks, stockists and direct ordering.

Bad Fads Museum
www.badfads.com
Revisit your past fashion mistakes.

BK Enterprises
www.b-k-enterprises.com
The only place to get that authentic 1970s Elvis jump suit. Prices range from $900 to $5000. Also has links to boot dealers, glasses shops and the place to get show scarves to complete the look.

Debenhams
www.debenhams.com
Indulge in some retail therapy at the site of everyone's favourite department store.

Diesel
www.diesel.co.uk
Browse their latest catalogue, hear music, and lots more – a very cool site. Also find time to check out the DieselKids games site, at: www.protokid.com

Enoki World
www.enokiworld.com
All the accessories you need for that vintage lifestyle: Pucci dresses, jadeite juicers, Pierre Cardin pink tweed skirts, 60s Gucci handbags.

FashionBot
www.fashionbot.com
Search several UK high-street retailers' catalogues.

fashion & beauty

Fashion Icon
www.fashion-icon.com
Irreverent New York fashion zine.

Fashion Information
www.fashioninformation.com
Pay for trend-forecasting reports.

Fashion Net
www.fashion.net
Handy shortcut to the highest-profile shopping, designer, magazine, modelling and fashion industry sites, with enough editorial to warrant an extended stopover.

Fashion UK
www.fuk.co.uk
Minimal but fresh vanity monthly from London.

Figleaves.com
www.figleaves.com
Online underwear superstore for both men and women. And the chaps can find a whole lot more at:
www.hom-fashion.co.uk

Firstview
www.firstview.com
See what's trotting the catwalks – sometimes at a price. For more previews, seek out Virtual Runway:
www.virtualrunway.com

Fragrance Direct

www.fragrancedirect.co.uk

It may look like a site for kids, but this etailer offers tremendous bargains on a good range of perfumes, cosmetics and skincare products.

Moda Italia

www.modaitalia.net

Patch through to the Italian rag traders.

Net-à-Porter

www.net-a-porter.com

Can't get to Harvey Nicks? Try here for posh frocks and accessories: Bottega Veneta, Clements Ribeiro, Missoni, Fake London and Paul & Joe are some of the cult labels this site stocks. Plus there's no snooty attitude. For Marc Jacobs, Fendi and Louis Vuitton, try:

www.eluxury.com

www.yoox.com

Organization for the Advancement of Facial Hair

www.ragadio.com/oafh

Includes an archive of classic beard styles and a library of grooming tips. For more advice on beard trimmers and how to keep your hulihee at its best (or just to see pics of guys who look like 1970s country singers), try these other hirsute sites:

www.badburns.com

www.beards.org

www.menwholooklikekennyrogers.com

Fig. 411	Fig. 359	Fig. 397	Fig. 388
Hollywoodian	Mutton Chops	A la Souvarov	French Fork

fashion & beauty

osMoz
www.osmoz.com
They haven't invented scratch'n'sniff technology for the Web yet, but this French site (in English) is the next best thing. A fragrance test will tell you whether floral or hesperide scents suit you best, and if you register they will send you free samples.

Salonweb
www.salonweb.com
Frizzy, flyaway, mousy, permed hair? Try this haircare portal for all the tips and advice you'll ever need. And for products visit:
www.4yourhair.co.uk
www.ehaircare.co.uk
www.hairways.net

Solemates: The Century in Shoes
www.centuryinshoes.com
Stepping out in the twentieth century.

Studs And Spikes
www.studsandspikes.com
Relive those glory days with your old leather jacket.

Style.com
www.style.com
With an impressive archive of images from all the major catwalk shows of the past two years, the online home of American *Vogue* is one of the best resources for fashionistas. If you're after a more standard magazine approach, try the British equivalent:
www.vogue.co.uk

Style Maven
www.stylemaven.com
Your guide to hip boutiques in London, New York, LA and San Francisco.

Textile Dictionary
www.ntgi.net/ICCF&D/textile.htm
Don't know your buckram from your qiviut? Check here.

Mullets

The Kentucky Waterfall, the Soccer Rocker, the Missouri Compromise, Business Up Front/Party In The Back, Neck Blanket, Ape Drape – whatever you want to call it, no hairstyle in the history of the civilized world has generated so much scorn, derision or passion as the mullet. Here are a few sites where you can mull over "the hairstyle of the gods":

Mullet Junky www.mulletjunky.com
Mullet Lovers www.mulletlovers.com
Mullet Madness www.mulletmadness.com
Mullets Galore www.mulletsgalore.com
Rate My Mullet www.ratemymullet.com

Victoria's Secret
www.victoriassecret.com
Order online or request the catalogue preferred by nine out of ten teenage boys.

Zoom
www.zoom.co.uk
Portal for the Arcadia group shops (Dorothy Perkins, Top Shop, Principles, Burton Menswear, etc), allowing you to re-create your high-street experience on the information superhighway.

Film

When it comes to movies, one site clearly rules:

The Internet Movie Database www.imdb.com

To say that it's impressive is an understatement. You'll be hard-pressed to find any work on or off the Net as comprehensive as this exceptional relational database of screen trivia from over 100,000 movies and a million actors. It's all tied together remarkably well – for example, within two clicks of finding your favourite movie you can get full filmographies of anyone from the cast

film

or crew and then see what's in the cooker. Still, it's not perfect, or without competition. You'll find a similar service with superior biographies and synopses at the colossal:

All Movie Guide www.allmovie.com

Or for more Chan, Li and Fat:

Hong Kong Movie Database www.hkmdb.com

For cinema listings:

Cinemas Online www.cinemas-online.co.uk
Cineworld www.cineworld.co.uk
Odeon www.odeon.co.uk
Picture House www.picturehouses.co.uk
UCI Cinemas www.uci-cinemas.co.uk
Virgin Net www.virgin.net/movies
Vue Cinemas www.myvue.com

Ain't It Cool News
www.aintitcool.com
The movie news and gossip site that has Hollywood execs quaking in their boots. Founder Harry Knowles has been blamed several times when movies have tanked at the box office, and *Premiere* magazine has ranked him as one of Hollywood's most powerful people. More production gossip can be overheard at:
www.chud.com
www.corona.bc.ca/films
www.darkhorizons.com
www.imdb.com/Sections/Inproduction

asSeenonScreen
www.asos.com
Buy stuff you've seen on TV or in movies. For more, try:
www.movieprop.com
www.propstore.co.uk

The Astounding B Monster
www.bmonster.com
Excellent resource for fans of Mamie Van Doren, Rondo Hatton and other cult 1950s and 1960s drive-in/late-show fodder. For fans of more modern fare like *Cannibal Women in the Avocado Jungle of Death*, there's:
www.badmovieplanet.com
www.stomptokyo.com/badmoviereport
www.badmovies.org
www.ohthehumanity.com

Atom Films
www.atomfilms.com
Watch entertaining short films. For sixteen-colour silliness see:
www.pixelfest.com

Bad Movie Night
www.hit-n-run.com
Invite a couple of mates over to your house, get in a few beers, rent an aggressively mediocre movie and hurl invective at the screen. More snide remarks available at:

film

http://bigempire.com/filthy
www.mrcranky.com
www.thestinkers.com

Blaxploitation.com
www.blaxploitation.com
Superfly guys and gals stickin' it to the man. More Afros and dashikis at BadAzz Mofo:
www.badazzmofo.com

Blooper Files
www.blooperfiles.com
Archive of screw-ups and inconsistencies from Hollywood's finest.
More continuity errors at:
www.movie-mistakes.co.uk
www.nitpickers.com

Bollywood World
www.bollywoodworld.com
Massive portal for the Indian film industry, with everything from production news to ringtones for your mobile.

British Film Institute
www.bfi.org.uk
Reviews, features and loads of great content.

CapAlert
www.capalert.com
To really unveil box-office evil. More to be found at:
www.screenit.com

Carfax-Abbey Horror Film Database
www.carfax-abbey.com
Splatter-flick Central, with loads of info on gore masters such as
Dario Argento and Wes Craven. More zombies and fake blood at:
www.joblo.com/arrow
www.dune12.demon.co.uk
www.sexgoremutants.co.uk

Dogme95
www.dogme95.dk
Homepage of the Danish film movement led by Lars Von Trier,
including the manifesto, a how-to page and the latest news from the
film vanguard.

Drew's Script-O-Rama
www.script-o-rama.com
Hundreds of entire film and TV scripts. Need help writing or selling
your own? Try:
www.scriptfly.com

DVD File
www.dvdfile.com
All the latest UK DVD release news and reviews. For more on DVD
hardware and software:
www.dvdtimes.co.uk

E! Online
www.eonline.com
Daily film and TV gossip, news and reviews.

film

Empire Magazine
www.empireonline.co.uk
Reviews of every film showing in the UK.

555-LIST
http://home.earthlink.net/~mthyen
Catalogue of fake telephone numbers used in TV and film.

Golden Raspberry Award Foundation
www.razzies.com
The Oscars in an alternate universe.

Hollywood Reporter
www.hollywoodreporter.com
Tinseltown tattle, loads of previews and reviews daily, plus a flick biz directory.

Home Cinema Choice
www.homecinemachoice.com
In-depth reviews of DVD players, LCD screens and generally the kind of entertainment hardware that would negate the need ever to leave your house again.

In-Movies
www.in-movies.com
If you've got broadband access you can watch trailers and short films. For more shorts and trailers:
www.britshorts.com
www.movie-trailers.com
www.sightsound.com

Melon Farmer's Video Hits
www.dtaylor.demon.co.uk
Challenges British screen censorship.

Movie Cliches
www.moviecliches.com
Nothing unfamiliar.

MovieFlix
www.movieflix.com
Download hundreds of movies, some free but most require a monthly subscription of $6.95.

MovieLens
http://movielens.umn.edu
Become a member of this site and it will give you movie recommendations based on your tastes. It may be a bit of a behavioural research exercise, but it's still a pretty neat way of avoiding video-shop malaise. Another site plays it safe:
www.filmsite.org

Moviemags.com
www.moviemags.com
Directory of film print and e-zines.

Movie Review Query Engine
www.mrqe.com
This specialist search engine, dedicated to finding film reviews on the Web, has a database of more than 25,000 titles and does an excellent job of finding info on obscure movies. But perhaps you'd prefer a summary:
www.rottentomatoes.com
www.filmreview.co.uk
http://film.guardian.co.uk

Movies.com
www.movies.com
Preview box-office features and trailers direct from the major studios. Loads more to be streamed at:
www.universalstudios.com
http://movies.real.com

Mr Kiss Kiss Bang Bang
www.ianfleming.org
An outrageously complete and obsessive guide to the shaken, not stirred universe of James Bond, with daily news and rumour updates.

film

Loads of companies are starting to do this now, even biggies such as **Amazon**. The basic idea is simple: you choose what you want to watch online, they post it to you, you watch it, you post it back ... easy. Some firms offer a flat-rate monthly membership which gives you a certain number of films each month, which could be a little restricting, so shop around for a deal that suits you. Here are a few of the best:

Blockbuster www.blockbuster.co.uk
DVDs 365 www.dvds365.com
LoveFilm.com www.lovefilm.com
Mailbox Movies www.mailboxmovies.com
Screen Select www.screenselect.co.uk

My Movies
www.mymovies.net
Huge film site with production news, gossip, reviews, competitions, shopping, trailers and, if you've got broadband, you can take advantage of the movies on demand.

SciFi.com
www.scifi.com
Science fiction news, reviews and short films. More of that sort of thing here:
http://scifi.ign.com
www.cinescape.com

Sendit
www.sendit.com
This is perhaps the best British DVD and video shop on the Net: good selection, excellent search facility and great prices. Other video and DVD etailers worth checking out are:
www.bensonsworld.co.uk
www.dvdpricesearch.com
www.dvdworld.co.uk
www.formovies.com

Shooting People
http://shootingpeople.org
In their own words, "the fastest growing UK online filmmakers' community"; whether you're a director without a crew, or runner with nowhere to run, look here first.

The Silents Majority
www.silentsmajority.com
This great online journal devoted to silent film is certainly one of the best film sites on the Web, even if you don't know Fatty Arbuckle from ZaSu Pitts. Even more silent wonders at:
www.silentera.com

Smoking List Movie Reviews
http://SmokingSides.com/asfs/m
A history of smoking on the silver screen. Non-smokers might want to try Soup at the Movies:
www.soupsong.com/imovies.html

Variety
www.variety.com
Screen news fresh off the PR Gatling gun.

VCR Repair Instructions
www.fixer.com
How to take a VCR apart and then get all the little bits back in so it fits easier into the bin.

Warning6
www.cinepad.com/warning6.htm
If you don't want to know the twists at the end of *The Usual Suspects* or *The Crying Game*, don't you dare visit this site.

Lo-tech film re-makes

Who needs a £20 million special effects and pyrotechnics budget when you've got a couple of Lego sets?

Being Puffy www.urbanentertainment.com/2
The Fountainhead – A Parody www.jeffcomp.com/faq/parody
Custom Star Wars Minifigs http://members.aol.com/jmacroy/update/legos/customs.html
Lego Star Wars Trilogy www.tanukikoji.or.jp/yes/lsw
Monty Python & the Holy Grail www.spiteyourface.com/python.html
Shark Attack www.exposure.co.uk/eejit/3act/sharkattack.html
Titanic Legos at Sea www.prtc.net/~kisspr/index2.htm

WildestWesterns.com
www.wildestwesterns.com
A great site for fans of classic oaters.

Food & Drink

African Studies Cookbook
www.sas.upenn.edu/African_Studies/Cookbook
A frighteningly comprehensive database of African recipes.

Al Mashriq
http://almashriq.hiof.no/general/600/640/641/recipes/misc.html
No-nonsense list of Middle Eastern recipes.

BBC Food
www.bbc.co.uk/food
A very branded site (there are lots of familiar faces) but with a good database of solid recipes that you can be sure will have been tested properly.

Beershots
http://micro.magnet.fsu.edu/beershots
Beers of the world put under a microscope.

Berry Brothers & Rudd
www.bbr.co.uk
Although the site looks a little intimidating, don't be put off: this is one of the country's best wine-ordering services. You can pick up bottles for around £6, although at the other end the sky's the limit. Try also:
www.oddbins.co.uk
www.virginwines.com

Bevnet
www.bevnet.com
"The beverage industry's source for product reviews, news & more."

Cheese
www.cheese.com
Excellent cheese information site with an exhaustive list of cheeses and detailed info on composition.

Cheeseburger in Paradise
www.fdu.com/cburger.htm
Stranded in Alabama or Helsinki and jonesing for a cheeseburger? Check here for your nearest vendor.

food & drink

Chile-Heads
www.exit109.com/~mstevens/chileheads.html
Get 'em while they're hot; more belly-burners at:
www.ringoffire.net

Chinatown
www.chinatown-online.co.uk/pages/food
Good site for Chinese recipes, information on ingredients and contextual stuff.

Chocolate Lover's Page
http://chocolocate.com
The good gear: where to find
recipes and dealers. And if just
looking at that site doesn't make
you pile on the pounds, visit:
www.chocolate.co.uk
www.divinechocolate.com
www.hotelchocolat.com

Cigar Aficionado
www.cigaraficionado.com
Archives, shopping guides and
tasting forums from the US glossy
that sets the benchmark in cigar
ratings. Modelled on:
www.crackaficionado.com

Cocina Mexicana
http://cocinamexicana.com.mx/ingles/menu/frame.html
A great site devoted to authentic Mexican cuisine ... unfortunately,
it's in Spanish.

Cocktail Time
www.cocktailtime.com
Guzzle your way to a happier home. Yes, do buy the book.
www.webtender.com
www.barmeister.com
www.drinkboy.com

Coffee Geek
http://coffeegeek.com
Everything caffeinated. For essential espresso links, see:
www.espressotop50.com
And for even more of the brown stuff:
www.coffeeuniverse.com
www.coffeefest.com

Cook's Thesaurus
www.foodsubs.com
Look no further if you want to find substitutes for fatty, expensive or
hard-to-find ethnic ingredients.

Cucina Direct
www.cucinadirect.co.uk
Excellent online kitchen equipment site with a solid bricks-and-
mortar business behind it.

Curryhouse
www.curryhouse.co.uk
Make the perfect vindaloo or look up your nearest balti house if
you're too lazy. For more masala matters, try:
http://rubymurray.com

Delia Online
www.deliaonline.com
A double-header of a site: lots of good recipes and useful tips plus
the alarming Delia diary for true fans who really want to know about
her life. And to see where all the site's ideas came from, go to:
www.marthastewart.com

Dolce Vita
www.dolcevita.com/cuisine
Life is sweet at this Italian cookery site.

The Empty Bowl
www.emptybowl.com
"The definitive source for all your cereal needs."

food & drink

Epicurious
www.epicurious.com
The best food website there is. Online marriage of Condé Nast's *Gourmet*, *Bon Appetit*, and *Traveler* magazines, crammed with recipes, culinary forums and advice on dining out worldwide.

Fair Trade on-line
www.fairtradeonline.com
Buy ethically traded food and drink from this site run by Traidcraft and Oxfam. For more on Fairtrade in the UK, see:
www.fairtrade.org.uk

Famers' Markets
www.farmersmarkets.net
Find your nearest farmers' market and start buying local food.

Food Allergy and Anaphylaxis Network
www.foodallergy.org
All the news and developments from the nut intolerance frontline.

Foodlink
www.foodlink.org.uk
Your complete guide to food safety. But if you can't remember anything about food safety unless it's set to music, go to:
http://foodsafe.ucdavis.edu/music.html

FoodnDrink
www.foodndrink.co.uk
A useful site with an online version of *Harden's Restaurant Guide* (created by people rather than food critics) and a restaurant booking facility, through 5pm (see link below). There are also links to shopping sites, a gourmet bookshop and a good cookery school directory.
www.5pm.co.uk

Fruitarian Site
www.fruitarian.com
The joys of chomping on raw fruit and the chance to make new fruitarian friends.

Generic Mac and Cheese Gallery
www.geocities.com/macandcheesebox
Gawp in wonder at the diet of the American student.

Good Pub Guide
www.goodguides.com
Offers a good pub locator for the UK, as if you needed help.

Internet Chef
www.ichef.com
Over 30,000 recipes, cooking hints ("Ground Beef Meals"), kitchen talk and more links than you can jab a fork at.

Jamie Oliver
www.jamieoliver.net
The most overexposed man on TV – but he makes a great salad.

Lakeland
www.lakelandlimited.co.uk
Everything you could and couldn't possibly need in the kitchen.

Leaping Salmon
www.leapingsalmon.co.uk
Quality prepared food that you simply assemble according to instructions – barely a chopping board required, and excellent food to boot. If you get the munchies in the middle of the night and need food cooked to order delivered to your door, try Room Service:
www.roomservice.co.uk

Meals For You
www.mealsforyou.com
A decent American recipe search engine – each listing includes the details of the fat and cholesterol present in each recipe.

New York Seafood
www.nyseafood.org
Great site for loads of piscine information. To get cod and haddock delivered to your door, try The Fish Society:
www.thefishsociety.co.uk

food & drink

Specialist shopping sites

Club Chef Direct www.clubchefdirect.co.uk
Suppliers of restaurant-quality meat, fish and produce.

Cyber Candy www.cybercandy.com
Brilliant site for exploring candy from all over the world – great for US and Japanese expats looking for a sugary flavour of home.

Fifth Sense www.fifthsense.com
An excellent site if you want to experiment a bit with spices or sauces from around the globe – mostly dry or bottled goods, though.

Fortnum & Mason www.fortnumandmason.com
Excellent luxury food shopping site sensibly separated into goods that can be sent in the UK only and those worldwide.

Marchents www.marchents.com
A good site that offers food delivery on everything from meat to veg, plus there's kitchen kit to buy too.

Real Meat www.realmeat.co.uk
A decent site that sells very good products – the firm behind the site is well known in foodie circles for producing top-notch flesh.

Thorntons www.thorntons.co.uk
Yummy chocolates and the site ain't bad either: easy to shop, with lots of gift ideas.

An Ode to Olives
www.emeraldworld.net/olive.html
You'll never look at an olive ambivalently again.

Oreo Stuff
www.jeffmajor.com/oreos
Someone with way too much time on his hands.

Our Food
www.ourfood.com
An excellent collection of scientific articles pertaining to food science and food safety.

Ray's List of Weird and Disgusting Foods
www.weird-food.com
How many have you tried?

Real Beer
www.realbeer.com
None of the usual beer yarns like waking up in a strange room stark-naked with a throbbing head and a hazy recollection of pranging your car. Here beer is treated with the same dewy-eyed respect usually reserved for wine and trains. Like to send your chum a virtual beer? Stumble over to:
www.pubworld.co.uk

Eating out

The AA www.theaa.co.uk
Decent search engine for nationwide restaurants and pubs.

Grabameal www.grabameal.co.uk
A database of over 23,000 restaurants and takeaways in the UK.

Square Meal www.squaremeal.co.uk
One of the better restaurant finders, plus news and views from the dining world.

This Is London www.thisislondon.co.uk
The *Evening Standard* site is the best for searching for bars and pubs and restaurants in London: comprehensive and with good-length reviews so you have an idea of exactly what you'll be getting.

Time Out http://eatdrink.timeout.com
Frequently updated rundown of London eateries, searchable by area or cuisine.

Toptable www.toptable.co.uk
No-nonsense site that covers London and some surrounding areas.

Zagats www.zagats.com
Excellent search engine for restaurant reviews the world over, plus restaurant news.

food & drink

Recipe Link
www.recipelink.com
Points to more than 10,000 galleries of gluttony.

Recipe Search
www.birdseye.com/search.html
Cast your line into the fishfinger king's own recipe database or trawl through hundreds of other Net collections. See also:
http://recipes.alastra.com
www.mealsforyou.com

Restaurant Row
www.restaurantrow.com
Key in your dining preferences and find the perfect match from hundreds of thousands of food barns worldwide.

Scope GM Food
http://scope.educ.washington.edu/gmfood
Forums, FAQs, links and reference library concerning mutant seeds.

ScotchWhisky.com
www.scotchwhisky.com
Excellent site with loads of info on whisky, plus a shopping facility.

Spice Advice
www.spiceadvice.com
Encyclopedia of spices covering their origins, purposes, recipes and tips on what goes best with what.

Tasty Insect Recipes
www.ent.iastate.edu/misc/insectsasfood.html
Dig in to such delights as Bug Blox, Banana Worm Bread, Rootworm Beetle Dip and Chocolate Chirpie Chip Cookies (with crickets).

Tea & Sympathy
http://pages.ripco.net/~c4ha2na9/tea
For more, try the Tea Council or, to buy tea, the English Tea Store:
www.teacouncil.co.uk
www.englishteastore.com

food & drink

Thai Recipes
www.importfood.com/recipes.html
Order fresh Thai produce, buy Thai cookware, dive in to recipes such
as Volcano Chicken or Frog with Chilli Paste, and sign up to a recipe
newsletter.

Tokyo Food Page
www.bento.com
Where and what to eat in Tokyo, plus recipes. More at:
www.thesushibar.com
www.sushilinks.com

Top Secret Recipes
www.topsecretrecipes.com
At least one commercial recipe, such as KFC coleslaw, revealed each
week. Many are surprisingly basic. Also investigate Copykat.com:
www.copykat.com

Buying groceries online

Buying food online is a very real option these days, even in most rural areas.
You might even find that delivery is free if you place a sizeable order. Many
of the big supermarkets offer online shopping:

Asda www.asda.co.uk
Iceland www.iceland.co.uk
Ocado (Waitrose) www.ocado.com
Sainsburys www.sainsburys.co.uk
Tesco www.tesco.co.uk

Or you could go for an organic delivery – which you'll find surprisingly good-
value compared to the organic offerings in the supermarkets. There are
nationwide schemes such as Simply Organic and Organic Shop, and the Soil
Association has a directory of local schemes and suppliers.

Organic Delivery www.organicdelivery.co.uk
Planet Organic www.planetorganic.com
Simply Organic www.simplyorganic.net
Soil Association www.soilassociation.org

Tudocs
www.tudocs.com
Rates cooking links across the web. Search under "fruit", for instance, and get linked to such ever-useful sites as 104 Things to Do With a Banana.

The Ultimate Cookbook
www.ucook.com
Pinch recipes from hundreds of popular cookbooks. More food porn unplugged at:
www.cook-books.com

WELCOME TO

Vegetarian Society of the UK
www.vegsoc.org
Support for veggies. And to find out where to eat without meat, try:
www.veggieheaven.com

Wine Spectator
www.winespectator.com
Research your hangover.

Furniture & Interiors

BBC Good Homes
www.beeb.com/goodhomes
The BBC's interiors magazine has all the features you've come to expect, offering advice on everything from Moroccan living rooms to the good flooring guide.

DesignBoom
www.designboom.com
Massive site with details of loads of design events worldwide. There's also a wealth of articles and potted histories.

furniture & interiors

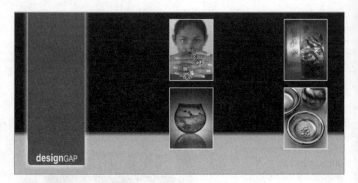

Design Gap
www.design-gap.co.uk
Directory of work by three hundred contemporary British designers and furniture makers that includes everything from tchotchkes to chests-of-drawers.

Design-Online
www.design-online.co.uk
A database of British interior designers, feng shui consultants, building services, soft furnishing companies and other providers of interiors essentials.

Furniture Guide
www.furnitureguide.com
Very impressive site covering all aspects of furniture, with glossaries, buying guides, shop locator, articles, style guide, etc.

Furniture Wizard
www.furniturewizard.com
Tips on how to restore your Louis XIV chair after your cat pees on it.

Geomancy.Net – The Centre for Applied Feng Shui Research
www.geomancy.net
Harmonize Qi and re-create the ambience of a Chinese restaurant. For more wizard assistance, try Qi Whiz and Feng Shui Fanzine: www.qi-whiz.com

furniture & interiors

History of Furniture Timeline
http://maltwood.finearts.uvic.ca/hoft
Detailed history of furniture, with glossary and links.

Let's Go Retro
www.letsgoretro.com
Get a Space Invaders machine for your living room.

Nubold.com
www.nubold.com
Home of lighting, glass, ceramics and tableware from contemporary designers like Bodo Sperlein and Nic Wood. They even offer a wedding-list service for couples with impeccable taste.

On-Line Furniture Style Guide
www.connectedlines.com/styleguide
Detailed guide to styles from Jacobean to Scandinavian.

Sotheby's Collecting Guides
www.sothebys.com
The venerable auction house's guides to collecting ceramics, furniture, prints, rugs, clocks and silver are well worth a gander.

Tribu-Design
www.tribu-design.com/en
A fascinating database of twentieth-century furniture and design.

Wallpaper Direct
www.wallpaperdirect.co.uk
Apparently wallpaper hasn't been this trendy since the 1970s, so stock up at this easy-to-use site, featuring a database of 20,000 papers, borders and fabrics.

The Work of Charles and Ray Eames
http://lcweb.loc.gov/exhibits/eames
The Library of Congress's online exhibition of the work of the most influential designers of the twentieth century.

Games

Most multiplayer games can be played across the Net. There are also thousands of simple table, word, arcade and music games as diverse as Chess, Blackjack, Connect 4, and Frogger that can be played on the Web courtesy of Java and Shockwave. In some cases you can even contest online opponents for prizes. Peruse the selection on offer at:

Coffee Break Arcade www.coffeebreakarcade.com
Flash Kit www.flashkit.com
Flazoom www.flazoom.com
Flipside www.flipside.com
FreeArcade.com www.freearcade.com
Gamesville www.gamesville.com
Playsite www.playsite.com
Pogo.com www.pogo.com
Shockwave.com www.shockwave.com
The Station www.station.sony.com
Yahoo! Games http://games.yahoo.com

For reviews, news, demos, hints, patches, cheats, downloads and other console, PC and Mac game necessities, try:

Absolute Playstation www.absolute-playstation.com
Avault www.avault.com
Gamers.com www.gamers.com
Games Domain www.gamesdomain.co.uk
Games Spot www.gamespot.com
Games Spy www.gamespy.com
HappyPuppy www.happypuppy.com
Hot Games www.hotgames.com
MacGamer www.macgamer.com
Old Man Murray www.oldmanmurray.com

PSXExtreme www.psxextreme.com
Total Games www.totalgames.net
XBox http://xbox.ign.com

Blues News
www.bluesnews.com
Keep up with what's Quakin'.

Cheat Station
www.cheatstation.com
Get Sonic to do what you want him to do. For more devious tricks,
try The Codebook:
www.codebook.se

ContestGuide
www.contestguide.com
Get junkmail for life by entering loads of competitions. More here:
www.contestlistings.com
www.uggs-n-rugs.com.au/contests

Croft Times
www.cubeit.com/ctimes
More news about the Tomb Raider bombshell than you could ever
want. For the truly smitten, you can download a customized version
of Internet Explorer featuring Lara's likeness everywhere.

Freeloader
www.freeloader.com
Download free games (such as Grand Theft Auto and Hidden &
Dangerous) for your PC. The catch: you have to look at ads ... lots of
ads.

Game Downloads
www.fileplanet.com
Stock up on even more gaming software.

GameFAQs
www.gamefaqs.com
Stuck on a level or just want to know more?

games

Game Girlz
www.gamegirlz.com
Team up with other game grrls and prepare to kick dweeb-boy butt right across their own turf. More reinforcement at:
www.womengamers.com

Gameplay
www.gameplay.com
Fifteen years old and still going strong, this is certainly the best British gaming portal, with an excellent magazine, shop and loads of online gaming options. For cheats, links and lower prices, check out:
www.ukgames.com

Gaming Age
www.gaming-age.com
All the latest news from the gaming frontline, plus interviews with designers and previews of big games before they hit the shops.

Kasparov Vs. The World
http://classic.zone.msn.com/kasparov
Take tips from the Russian master.

Pointless Games
http://pointlessgames.com
A selection of games that are actually worse than Pong.

Popex
www.popex.com
Similar to Fantasy Football or Fantasy Shares, but with pop bands.

RPG Vault
http://rpgvault.ign.com
Role Playing Gamers' heaven.

Text-Based Pong
www.karber.net/textbased/pong/default.htm
Pong – the first and simply the greatest computer game. This is the oddest version you'll ever play.

Vintage Gaming
www.vg-network.com
Revive old-school arcade games such as Xevious on your home PC. For more 1980s fun, try:
www.emuunlim.com
www.smiliegames.com

Gardening

The Botanical Dermatology Database
http://bodd.cf.ac.uk
Why you should wear gardening gloves.

British Trees
www.british-trees.com
Dedicated to the preservation of British woodland.

The Carnivorous Plant FAQ
www.sarracenia.com/faq.html
Novel solutions for garden pests.

gardening

Crocus
www.crocus.co.uk
The main draw of this online garden centre is that plants are delivered by trained gardeners who will help bolster your borders. There are also sections devoted to plant finding, jargon busting and news and advice on organic gardening.

Dig It
www.dig-it.co.uk
Comprehensive gardening site, including a shopping service where everything is allegedly sourced from environmentally friendly companies, a good magazine section and a facility to email the site's experts. For more, see Just Gardeners:
www.justgardeners.com

English Country Gardening
www.suite101.com/welcome.cfm/english_country_gardening
Jane Hollis's site devoted to the grand old art of English country gardening includes discussion groups, articles, virtual tours and flower show and garden reports.

Garden Forum
www.gardenforum.co.uk
All the latest news, views, advice, job postings and gossip from the gardening community.

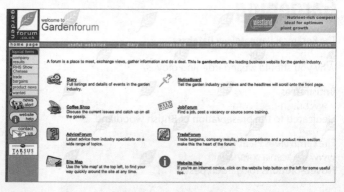

Garden Guides
www.gardenguides.com
Has most of the features you should expect from the better general
gardening sites (plant guides, discussion forums, advice), but this
site sets itself apart with its lengthy book extracts on topics like
choosing bulbs and designing herb gardens.

Garden Visit
www.gardenvisit.com
Maps of gardens open to the public around the world and a history
of garden design.

Garden Web
www.gardenweb.com
One of the best horticultural resources on the Web, this site hosts
a multitude of regional and specialist forums (roses, wild flowers,
kitchen gardens), plus a glossary, plant database, calendar of events,
plant and seed exchange, plenty of articles and shopping areas.

Growing Lifestyle
www.growinglifestyle.com
A dedicated home-and-garden search engine.

Kitchen Gardener
www.taunton.com/finegardening
Online presence of *Kitchen Gardener* magazine, dedicated to foodies
who grow their own produce. For a more organic perspective, check
out:
www.thevegetablepatch.com

Open Directory Gardens
http://dmoz.org/Home/Gardens
The Open Directory Project's comprehensive set of links.

Postcode Plant Database
www.nhm.ac.uk/science/projects/fff
This excellent resource from the Natural History Museum allows you
to find the right native trees, shrubs and flowers for your area.

Royal Botanic Gardens
www.rbgkew.org.uk
Featuring access to its enormous academic database, the homepage
of Kew Gardens is one for the real horticulturalist.

Royal Horticultural Society
www.rhs.org.uk
The online presence of the RHS includes plant databases, seasonal
advice and a garden finder.

Gay & Lesbian

AEGIS
www.aegis.com
Claiming to be the largest HIV/AIDS related site on the Web, AEGIS is
an amazing resource filled with the latest news from the treatment
front, bulletin boards, a law library of judicial cases and an archive
of publications from organizations such as Gay Men's Health Crisis
and Act Up, and from the Government. For more news, advice and
dispatches from the activist front, try:
www.gmhc.org
www.actupny.org

The AIDS Memorial Quilt
www.aidsquilt.org
View the quilt online, find out how to become involved with the
project, and contribute to the memory book.

Gay.com UK
http://uk.gay.com
The British version of the enormous American portal has a huge
array of channels for everyone from scene queens to those not yet
out of the closet. Also see:
www.planetout.com
www.queertheory.com

Gay Britain Network

www.gaybritain.co.uk

Homepage of the network that hosts sites such as UK Gay Shopping, UK Gay Guide and Gay Video Shop.

Gay & Lesbian Alliance against Defamation

www.glaad.org

Stand up against media stereotyping and discrimination against those deviating from the heterosexual norm.

Gayscape

www.gayscape.com/gayscape

Probably the best gay search engine on the Web. See also the Queer Resource Directory, the Gay Index and Larry-bob's:

www.qrd.org

www.gayindex.co.uk

www.io.com/~larrybob/hotlist.html

Gay to Z

www.gaytoz.com

Directory of gay-friendly hotels, bars, clubs, builders, plumbers, electricians and erotica in London, Manchester and Brighton. Give them your email address and they'll send you more complete guides on the above cities plus Paris. For more hotels in the UK and abroad, try:

Gay Travel Guide

www.gaytravel.co.uk

This excellent site has detailed guides to destinations such as Mykonos, Benidorm, Ibiza, New York and Amsterdam, plus a good search facility for gay-friendly hotels in more exotic locales. Also see:

www.gayhotel.co.uk

Holy Titclamps

www.holytitclamps.com

Homepage of San Francisco's fab queer zine which features fiction by the likes of Sarah Schulmann and Steve Abbot plus comics, poetry, rants and humour from some of the best writers and artists on the scene.

gay & lesbian

Lesbian UK
www.lesbianuk.co.uk
A database of resources for Britain's lesbian community.

The Old Dyke
www.rowfant.demon.co.uk
Essays devoted to lesbian and women's history.

OUTintheUK
www.outintheuk.com
Fantastic, non-profit networking site for gay men who want to meet other gay men socially.

OutRage!
http://outrage.nabumedia.com
Peter Tatchell's organization fighting for equal rights and against assimilation into straight society.

Pink Passport
www.pinkpassport.com
A site with all the usual features, but it does have one of the best gay venue selectors on the Web, covering the entire world.

Stonewall
www.stonewall.org.uk
The homepage of the lesbian and gay rights organization may strike some as dull and worthy, but it's a good source of information on British activism and issues like the age of consent.

Techno Dyke
www.technodyke.com
Part of the Indie Gurl Network (www.indiegurl.com) of zines, this fun e-zine has drag king galleries, horoscopes, articles on sex and rela-tionships and a "Biosphere" section.

UK Gay Guide
www.gayguide.co.uk
The design is slightly irritating, but this site features excellent guides to UK gay-friendly services plus advice and personals.

Genealogy

Don't expect to enter your name and produce an instant family tree, but you might be able to fill in a few gaps.

Ancient Faces
www.ancientfaces.com
Picture your ancestors.

Cyndi's List
www.cyndislist.com
Twenty million users can't be wrong. With just about 100,000 links, the genealogy resource you're after is undoubtedly here. For Brit-specific links, try:
www.ukgenealogy.co.uk

Ellis Island Records
www.ellisislandrecords.org
If your family had a stopover in the US in the past 150 years or so, their records will be here.

Family History
www.familyhistory.com
This site, a section of the massive Ancestry.com umbrella, hosts some 130,000 message boards organized by surname or location. You can also set up your own family website here for free.

FamilySearch
www.familysearch.org
If you're going to be doing family research on the Web you'll come here at one stage or another. This site (also known as the LDS Resource) is run by the Mormons, who believe it is their duty to record the ancestry of every living soul. The religious aspect is played down in favour of sheer information.

Free Surname Search
www.freesurnamesearch.com
A global database of surnames that might be of some use. Also see:
www.surnameweb.org

Historical Text Archive
http://historicaltextarchive.com
A very useful resource for people with Caribbean and African ancestry, including a Caribbean ancestry newsletter and a database of slave names. Also check the Christine's Genealogy site:
http://ccharity.com

Public Record Office
www.nationalarchives.gov.uk
Not a great resource in itself, but if you need to approach the Public Record Office or National Archive for materials this site gives you the lowdown on how to go about it. More information can be found on the Government's Family Records site:
www.familyrecords.gov.uk

RootsWeb
www.rootsweb.com
The oldest, largest and probably the best free genealogy site on the Net. It features a very good search engine, links to resources and lots of humour preventing things from getting too dull. More gene gardening can be done at:
www.ancestry.com
www.familytreemaker.com
www.genhomepage.com
www.genealogytoday.com

Gossip & Celebrities

Every celebrity has at least one obsessive fan site in their honour, but finding them can sometimes be tricky. If they're not listed in **Yahoo!**, try:

Celebhoo www.celebhoo.com
CelebSites www.celebsites.com
Celebrity Site Of The Day www.csotd.com
Webring www.webring.org
Google Directory http://directory.google.com/Top/Arts/Movies

Search engines tend to find porn scuttlers who've loaded their HTML meta tags with celebrity names – easy bait, when you consider that most fans would be more than happy to catch a glimpse of their idol in various states of undress:

Celebrity Nudity Database www.cndb.com

If they succeed in catching your attention, at least have the sense not to pull out your credit card. Adding **-naughty -naked -nude** to your search term, or enabling an adult filter such as **Google**'s SafeSearch (under Preferences), might help weed them out.

ABC News Entertainment
http://abcnews.go.com:80/sections/entertainment
Rumours and legit showbiz news from one of America's big three TV networks.

Beat Box Betty
www.beatboxbetty.com
Gossip and industry news "with a twist of blonde".

Celebrity Baby Blog
http://celebritybabies.typepad.com
This blog is overflowing with snaps of celebrity tots, all the gossip surrounding them and, most importantly, what they are wearing this season.

Chic Happens
www.hintmag.com/chichappens/chichappens.php
Horacio Silva and Ben Widdicombe's superb gossip page.

gossip & celebrities

Cinescape
www.cinescape.com
The latest insider industry news. Not as good as *The Hollywood Reporter*, but you don't have to subscribe.

Coat Hangers of the Rich and Famous
www.geocities.com/hangmycoat
A revealing look inside the closet of some of the world's biggest stars.

Drudge Report
www.drudgereport.com
Rumours from inside the Washington Beltway with a distinctly right-wing slant, from the online columnist who almost brought down a president.

E! Online
www.eonline.com
The latest from the States courtesy of the homepage of the American cable TV channel.

Famous Birthdays
www.famousbirthdays.com
See who shares your birthday. As then see again at:
http://us.imdb.com/OnThisDay

Fanzine
www.fanzine.co.uk
The official addresses of stars and pop groups. For more direct
access, try Chip's Celebrity Home E-mail Addresses, and if that
doesn't land you with a restraining order, reach out to more stars at
Celebrity Addresses and Celebrity Email:
www.addresses.site2go.com
www.writetoaceleb.com
www.celebrityemail.com

Filth2Go
www.filth2go.com
Outrageous, scandal-
ous, rude gay gossip zine.
Unfortunately, you have to
subscribe.

Find a Grave
www.findagrave.com
See where celebrities are
buried.

Hello!
www.hellomagazine.co.uk
All the jet trash and desperate celebs you expect from the glossy,
only with lower production values. For an American version of the
same without the minor royalty, try:
http://people.aol.com

National Enquirer
www.nationalenquirer.com
All the news that's not fit to print elsewhere. Even less believable
"news" can be found at Weekly World News:
www.weeklyworldnews.com

gossip & celebrities

New York Post
www.nypostonline.com/gossip/gossip.htm
The latest dish from the columnists of the Big Apple's most notorious tabloid.

Popbitch
www.popbitch.com
Scurrilous, rude, fun and yes, downright bitchy, this is without question the best British pop gossip site. Their weekly mailing lists have brought down careers and halt work all over the capital every Thursday.

Pop Justice
www.popjustice.com
Fabulously bitchy site taking aim at the teen pop hordes.

The Smoking Gun
www.thesmokinggun.com
Tom Cruise's petition for divorce, Linda Fiorentino's nudity rider and other documents of celebrity misbehaviour.

TeenHollywood.com
www.teenhollywood.com
All the latest dirt and news on Tinseltown's pretty young things.

Variety
www.variety.com
Screen news fresh off the PR Gatling gun.

Health

While the Net's certainly an unrivalled medical library, it's also an unrivalled promulgator of the twenty-first-century equivalent of old wives' tales. So by all means research your ailment and pick up fitness tips online, but as the pill bottles say, check with your doctor before putting them to work. And while you're with your GP, ask if they use the Net for research and if so, which sites they recommend.

Don't expect to go online for first-aid advice. If it's an emergency, you won't have time. The Net is better for in-depth research and anecdotal advice, none of which comes quickly. But once you've spent a few sessions online studying your complaint, you'll be fully prepared to state your case. To find a doctor, dentist or specialist, try:

NetDoctor www.netdoctor.co.uk.

Or for a phone, fax or email response that could save your life on the road, try:

WorldClinic www.worldclinic.com

It's hard to say where to start your research. Perhaps a directory, or you could try one of the specialist health portals:

Health on the Net www.hon.ch
Hospitalweb UK www.hospitalweb.co.uk
MedExplorer www.medexplorer.com
Patient UK www.patient.co.uk
SearchBug www.searchbug.com/health

Or a government gateway:

NHS Direct www.nhsdirect.nhs.uk
World Health Organization www.who.int/home-page

health

You'll find tons of excellent self-help megasites, though the presence of sponsors may raise ethical questions. Their features vary, but medical encyclopedias, personal health tests and Q&A services are fairly standard fare. Starting with the former US Surgeon General's site, try:

Dr Koop www.drkoop.com
HealthAtoZ.com www.healthatoz.com
HealthCentral www.healthcentral.com
HealthWorld www.healthy.net
Intellihealth www.intellhealth.com
Mayo Clinic www.mayoclinic.com
Netdoctor.co.uk www.netdoctor.co.uk
Surgery Door www.surgerydoor.co.uk
24Dr.com www.24dr.com
WebMD www.webmd.com
WebMD (Lycos) http://webmd.lycos.com
Yahoo! Health http://health.yahoo.com

But for serious research go straight to **Medline**, the US National Library of Medicine's database. It archives, references and abstracts thousands of medical journals and periodicals going back to 1966. You can get it free at **PubMed**, but the subscription services may have access to more material. These are aimed more at health pros and students:

Medline Plus www.nlm.nih.gov/medlineplus
Medscape www.medscape.com
Ovid www.ovid.com
PubMed www.ncbi.nlm.nih.gov/PubMed

Despite first appearances, **Martindale**'s maintains an outstanding directory of medical science links:

Martindale's www.martindalecenter.com/HSGuide.html

If you know what you have and you want to contact other sufferers, use a search engine (www.google.com) or directory (http://dmoz.org) to find organizations and personal homepages. They should direct you to useful mailing lists and discussion groups. If not, try **Google Groups** (http://groups.google.com) to find the right newsgroups.

Acne Regimen
www.acne.org
Out, damned spot! Out …

Alex Chiu's Eternal Life Device
http://www.alexchiu.com
Live forever or come back for your money.

All Nurses
http://www.allnurses.com
Springboard to chat groups, research data, professional bodies, jobs and other nursing resources.

Ask Dr Weil
www.drweil.com
Popdoctor Andrew Weil's eagerness to prescribe from a range of bewildering and often conflicting alternative therapies has seen him called a quack in some quarters, but not by Warner. *Time* put him on the front cover and gave him a job peddling advice beside vitamin ads. Whether or not you believe in food cures, his daily Q&As are always a good read.

Biopharm Leeches
www.biopharm-leeches.com
Cure your ailments the old-fashioned way.

The British Chiropractic Association
www.chiropractic-uk.co.uk
Don't get bent out of shape: this is a good introduction to chiropractic health care.

Alternative medicines

Part of the Net's ongoing research function is the ability to contact people who've road-tested alternative remedies and can report on their efficacy. Try **Google Groups** or one of these links to work your way to an answer:

About http://altmedicine.about.com
AlternativeMedicine.com www.alternativemedicine.com
WholeHealthMD www.wholehealthmd.com
Alternative Dr www.alternativedr.com

For more specific cures, see:

Acupuncture.com
http://acupuncture.com
Probably the best and certainly the most comprehensive site dealing with Chinese medicine. As well as acupuncture, it covers Chinese herbal remedies, Qi Gong and Tui Na (massage) for patients, students and practitioners alike. For more information, try Oriental Medicine:
www.orientalmedicine.com

Aromatherapy
www.aromaweb.com
Pseudoscience it might be (http://skepdic.com/aroma.html), but you'll be on the way to smelling better. And surely that can't be a bad thing.

Medicinal Herb Faq
http://ibiblio.org/herbméd/faqs/medi-cont.html
If it's in your garden and it doesn't kill you, it can only make you stronger. More leafy cures and love drugs at:
www.herbal-ahp.org

ThinkNatural
www.thinknatural.com
Order homeopathic, herbal, Ayurvedic and Chinese remedies for next-day delivery, plus advice on how to use them properly.

The Yoga Site
www.yogasite.com
A good, general site on the various asanas and vinyasas so you can stretch yourself back into shape. For even more karma try:
www.holisticonline.com/Yoga/hol_yoga_home.htm
www.yoganation.com

Calorie Counter
www.caloriecounter.co.uk
Diet sensibly. For more dieting advice, check out the Open
Directory's Weight Loss pages:
http://dmoz.org/Health/Weight_Loss

CancerHelp UK
www.cancerhelp.org.uk
Jargon-free guide to living with the disease, plus information on
treatments, ongoing studies and trials.

Color Vision Test
www.umist.ac.uk/UMIST_OVS/UES/COLOUR0.HTM
Do you dress in the dark or are you merely colour-blind?

ConsumerLab
www.consumerlab.com
An independent testing authority which publishes its studies online.
It tests herbal remedies, vitamins, supplements, sports products
and functional foods for effectiveness, purity, potency, consistency
and bioavailability (ie, whether the body can deal with the product
properly).

The Diabetes Quiz
www.diabetes.co.il
How much do you know about the condition?

Dr Squat
www.drsquat.com
Avoid getting sand kicked in your face through full squats. Also see:
www.weightsnet.com

Embarrassing Problems
www.embarrassingproblems.com
Help with everything from anal itching to wind.

Gyro's Excellent Hernia Adventure
www.cryogenius.com/mesh
Holiday snaps from under the knife.

health

HandHeldMed
www.handheldmed.com
Arm your pocket computer with medical software and references.
There's even more to be found at:
http://medicalpocketpc.com
www.pdamd.com

Health Fitness Tips
www.health-fitness-tips.com
Ironically, the site itself is somewhat flabby, but hopefully the exercise tips, low-fat recipes and motivational quotes will help you shed the inches.

Internet Health Library
www.internethealthlibrary.com
Information on complementary therapy from the University of Essex.

Lab Tests
www.labtestsonline.org
Get inside your sample.

Drugs

Everything you ever wanted to know about the pleasure, pain and politics of psychoactive drugs and the cultures built around them:

Erowid www.erowid.org
Lycaeum www.lycaeum.org
Neuro Pharmacology www.neuropharmacology.com
Drug Library www.druglibrary.org

Mental Health
www.mentalhealth.com
It's guaranteed that you'll come out of this site convinced there's something wrong with you. Worry your way along to:
www.anxietynetwork.com

Museum of Questionable Medical Devices
www.mtn.org/quack
Gallery of health-enhancing products where even breaks weren't bundled free.

Violet Ray Generators

NOTICES OF JUDGEMENT

3458. Misbranding of violet ray device, S. v 2 Cases * * *. (F. D.C. No. 30801. Sample no. 3858-L.):

LIBEL FILED: Between March 2 and April 24, 1951, District of Maryland.

The device we are most often asked about is the Violet Ray Generator, sometimes called an "ultra violet device." Tens of thousands of these devices were sold for home use between about 1915 and 1950 under brand names such as Masters, Elco and Renulife. <u>Literature</u> accompanying the devices claimed to cure just about

health

National Institute of Ayurvedic Medicine
http://niam.com/corp-web
A good, low BS guide to balancing your life energies with the ancient Indian practice.

19th Century Medical Curios
www.zoraskingdom.freeserve.co.uk
The Elephant Man, bearded women and other strange Victoriana.

Nutritional Supplements
www.nutritionalsupplements.com
First-hand experiences with vitamins, body-building supplements, and other dubious health-shop fodder. For the real deal, go to the British Nutrition Foundation:
www.nutrition.org.uk

Quackwatch
www.quackwatch.com
Separating the docs from the ducks. Don't buy into any alternative remedies until you've read these pages.
www.ncahf.org
www.hcrc.org
http://nccam.nih.gov

Reuters Health
www.reutershealth.com
Medical newswires, reviews, opinion and reference.

RxList
www.rxlist.com
Look up your medication to ensure you're not being poisoned.

Spas Directory
www.thespasdirectory.com
Locate a British spa or health resort.

Talk Surgery
www.talksurgery.com
Discuss your operation with people who appear interested.

Travel Health
www.travelhealth.co.uk
Come back in one piece.

The Virtual Hospital
www.vh.org
Patient care and distance learning via online multimedia tools such as illustrated surgical walkthroughs.

The Visible Human Project
www.nlm.nih.gov/research/visible
Whet your appetite by skimming through scans of a thinly filleted serial killer, and then top it off with a fly-through virtual colonoscopy. For higher production values, see the Virtual Body:
www.medtropolis.com

Women's Health
www.bbc.co.uk/health/womens_health
A refreshingly relatively unbranded site from the Beeb.

World Wide Online Meditation Center
www.meditationcenter.com
Connect with your essence.

History

ArchNet
http://archnet.asu.edu
Digital directory to online archeology sites with an academic leaning. See also the Archaeological Resource Guide to Europe:
http://odur.let.rug.nl/arge

BBC Online – History
www.bbc.co.uk/history
As you'd expect, the Beeb's history pages are a good place to start.
They're well designed and informative – if a bit too traditional and
not as complete as you might like.

Britannia
http://britannia.com/history
One of the best British history sites on the Web, with biographies
of the "bravest knights of the fourteenth century", virtual tours of
Sussex churches, a history of Welsh royalty and an electronic version
of the Anglo-Saxon Chronicle.

History Buff
www.historybuff.com
A collection of press clippings through the ages.

History Channel
www.historychannel.com
This Web home of the American cable TV channel has perhaps too
much of an American slant for most British users, but it does have
some great features, such as an amazing archive of great speeches,
both as text and as RealAudio documents.

History House
www.historyhouse.com
Dedicated to rescuing history from the historians, this excellent
American site tells the stories of real people who have had an
impact on the world's major and not so major events. A necessary
corrective to the "great man of history" myths.

History Ring
http://members.tripod.com/~PHILKON/ring.html
Homepage of the history ring, linking you to hundreds and hundreds of non-commercial history sites.

Internet History Sourcebooks Project
www.fordham.edu/halsall
Professor Paul Halsall's site is a fantastic resource for students of history. His directory of Internet articles has links to thousands of articles on women's history, Jewish history, Islamic history, African history, lesbian and gay history, medieval studies and the more standard ancient and modern cultures.

Journal for Multimedia History
www.albany.edu/jmmh
Academic history journal with hyperlinked bells and whistles.

Regia Anglorum
www.regia.org
Relive the age of the Vikings.

Hobbies

All Magic Guide
www.allmagicguide.com
Your passport to the world of illusion.

Balloon HQ
www.balloonhq.com
Become a part of pop culture.

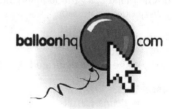

The Contortion Home Page
www.contortionhomepage.com
"Hey, Stretch, how do you do that?"

hobbies

Experimental Aircraft
http://exp-aircraft.com
Online resource for lunatics interested in building their own planes.

Firewalking.com
www.firewalking.com
The official website of Tolly Burkan, the father of firewalking.

Home Sewing Association
www.sewing.org
Pick up hints from a bunch of sew and sews.

International String Figure Association
www.isfa.org
Perfect your cat's cradle technique.

Joseph Wu's Origami Page
www.origami.vancouver.bc.ca
Gateway to the wide world of paper folding, including diagrams, galleries and links. To make your folds fly, see:
www.paperairplanes.co.uk

Juggling Information Service
www.juggling.org
If you can't keep your balls up, this site has just about everything any sane human could ever want to know about juggling. There's a collection of juggling software so you can see how the pros do it, a history of juggling and other arcane stuff. For the "best beanbag kit on the market", try the Juggling Store:
www.jugglingstore.com

Kitez
www.kitez.com
Go fly a kite at this dedicated search engine for kitesurfers.

Model Mart
www.modelmart.co.uk
Model online community for modellers.

NMRA Directory of World Wide Rail Sites
www.cwrr.com/nmra
The National Model Railroad Association's vast site of model railway links across the world.

Potato Cannon Fun Page
www.geocities.com/Yosemite/Rapids/1489
Charm and delight your parents for years to come.

The Puppetry Homepage
www.sagecraft.com/puppetry
The ups and downs from the world of puppetry, from animatronics to ventriloquism.

Rocketry.org
www.rocketry.org
Send your worst enemy to the Moon.

TreasureNet
www.treasurenet.com
Exchange tall tales and learn about metal detection.

Home Improvement

Ask the Master Plumber
www.clickit.com/bizwiz/homepage/plumber.htm
Save a small fortune by unblocking your own toilet.

B&Q
www.diy.com
B&Q's site may look like a Sunday paper pull-out ad, but there's plenty here. Also see Homebase:
www.homebase.co.uk

BarPlans
www.barplans.com
Move the Queen Vic into your basement.

Coping With Winter
www.ag.ndsu.nodak.edu/coping
Building a ski house in the Alps or moving to Irkutsk? Follow these building and DIY tips from North Dakota State University.

DIY Fix It
www.diyfixit.co.uk
This decent UK home improvement encyclopedia is very informative, and one of the few that come from this side of the pond.

Fine Homebuilding
www.taunton.com/home
American magazine for real DIY enthusiasts.

Fix it now
www.fixitnow.com
Battling with a washing machine or microwave? Help is at hand from the Samurai Appliance Repair Man. Also see:
www.repairclinic.com

Home Repair Stuff
www.factsfacts.com/MyHomeRepair
Design-free site answering questions such as "Which caulk?" and "Squirrel in your belfry?", plus beginner's guides and basic tool kits.

Home Tips
www.hometips.com
Load your toolbox, roll up your sleeves and prepare to go in. Then retreat, have a cup of tea, and take another look online. Try:
www.homestore.com
www.doityourself.com
www.naturalhandyman.com

How to Clean Anything
www.howtocleananything.com
Just add elbow grease.

home improvement

Improveline
www.improveline.com
Peruse the latest design ideas and find someone to do the job. You can even screen your local builders against public records and find the one least likely to quaff all your home brew and sell your nude holiday snaps to the *National Enquirer*. Also see:
www.homepro.com

ImproveNet
http://improvenet.com
Yankee DIY giant with more advice, calculators, shopping facilities and so on than any sane person can handle. It even includes archives from *Popular Mechanics* and *Today's Homeowner* as well as energy conservation articles, project guides and personal project managers.

MFI
www.mfi.co.uk
Redo your kitchen with some modular cabinets. For more chi-chi options, try Magnet and PS4 Kitchens:
www.magnet.co.uk
www.ps4kitchens.co.uk

The Old House Web
www.oldhouseweb.net
An excellent resource for those restoring the old money pit. Again, the site is American so the product info may not be entirely appropriate, but there are good articles on choosing the right primer and quick fixes for wallpaper repair problems.

ThePlumber.com
www.theplumber.com
Includes tips and online repair handbooks plus the history of plumbing from Babylonia through the inventions of Thomas Crapper to waterworks in the White House. For more plumbing sites, try the Plumbing Web:
www.plumbingweb.com

Self Build

www.selfbuildanddesign.com

If you'd rather build your own house than visit an estate agent, click here. Also try:

www.ebuild.co.uk

www.self-build.co.uk

Skills Register

www.skills-register.com

Thinking of hiring a plumber or handyman? Try this great service: a directory of British tradespeople who have passed site owner Will Stevens's stringent quality assurance tests. For a bigger database, try Improveline:

www.improveline.com

This to That

www.thistothat.com

So what would you like to glue today?

Wacky Uses

www.wackyuses.com

Using Coca-Cola to clean corrosion from batteries, pantyhose to polish furniture and other wacky household hints from Joey Green.

Horoscopes & Fortune-telling

800 Predict
www.800predict.com
Put your hands on your mouse for free psychic readings, love compatibility charts, daily lottery numbers, love casts and star gossip.

American Federation of Astrologers
www.astrologers.com
Impress your hairdresser by becoming a fully accredited seer by correspondence course.

Astro Advice
www.astroadvice.com
Aside from its treasure trove of arcane astrological systems (like Nine Star Ki) and slightly dodgy advice pages (astrological financial forecasts, for example), this site's best feature is its free, in-depth astrological charts.

Astrology.com
www.astrology.com
This sprawling site contains advice and predictions from just about every soothsaying system under the sun. There are horoscopes both free and charged, past-life reports, celebrity horoscopes, self-empowerment guides, karmic profiles, crystal balls, Chinese astrological readings and plenty more.

Astrology – Atlas and Time Zone Database
www.astro.com/cgi-bin/atlw3/aq.cgi?lang=e
Know exactly what was happening upstairs the second of your birth. Or if you prefer your cold readings, or with a touch less pseudoscientific mumbo-jumbo, try:
www.skepdic.com/coldread.html
http://astrology.about.com
www.astrocenter.com
www.skepdic.com/astrolgy.html

Psyche tests

Psyche Tests www.psychtests.com
Emode www.emode.com
Learner.org www.learner.org/exhibits/personality
Keirsey.com www.keirsey.com

So, what breed of dog are you? Smug sceptics (www.skepdic.com/myersb. html) say you'll get closer to the truth here:

Queendom.com www.queendom.com/tests.html

Biorhythm Generator
www.facade.com/attraction/biorhythm
Generate a cyclical report that can double as a sick note.

Dreamstop
www.dreamstop.com
Analyse your night visions and jot them into a journal to share with your friends.

horoscopes & fortune-telling

Metalog
www.astrologer.com
The home of the Astrological Association of Great Britain and the Centre for Psychological Astrology, this site "is devoted to promoting serious quality astrology; hopefully a place where many people will discover the richness of their own unique chart and learn that they are more than 'just' their sun-sign."

Oracle of Changes
www.iching.com
This excellent site enables you to consult virtually the I Ching, the ancient Chinese book of divination and soothsaying. The user casts coins into a pool six times which creates a hexagram that the oracle interprets according to the laws of ancient wisdom. See also:
www.facade.com/Occult/iching

Panchang
www.panchang.com
Get a personalized time-planner based on this ancient Indian astrological system.

Past Life Regression
www.pastlives.cc
Send your worst enemy back to the Stone Age.

RealAge
www.realage.com
Compare your biological and chronological ages.

Russell Grant Astrology
www.live-astro.com/horoscopes
Chirpy, cheerful advice from the chubby prognosticator.

Sarena's Tarot Page
www.talisman.net/tarot
Look no further if you need help with your chandelier, fan or seven triplet spreads. Also, for the expert only, a section on tarot spells. Also consult Tarot Magi:
www.tarot.com

Spirit Network

http://spiritnetwork.com

Portal for horoscopes, psychic readings, biorhythms, I Ching readings, paranormal activity and other New Age pursuits.

Stichomancy

www.facade.com/stichomancy

Type in your question and the computer will choose a book and a passage at random that miraculously will apply to your query. See also Bibliomancy, which chooses Bible passages at random to aid you in your quest for the answers:

www.facade.com/bibliomancy

The Voice of the Woods

www.pixelations.com/ogham

This is the site to visit if you wish to seek guidance from the Ogham, an ancient Celtic divination method.

What's in your name?

www.kabalarians.com

The Kabalarians claim names can be boiled down to a numerical stew and served back up as a character analysis. Look yourself up in here and see what a duff choice your parents made. Then blame them for everything that's gone wrong since.

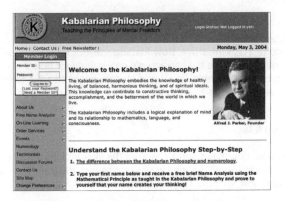

Kids & Teens

It's your choice whether to let them at it headlong or bridle their experience through rose-coloured filters. But if you need guidance or pointers towards the most kidtastic chowder, set sail into these realms:

Cybersmart Kids www.cybersmartkids.com.au
Internet Detectives www.madison.k12.wi.us/tnl/detectives
Kids Domain www.kidsdomain.com
NetMom www.netmom.com
Open Directory: Kids http://dmoz.org/Kids_and_Teens
Scholastic International www.scholastic.com
Surfing the Net with Kids www.surfnetkids.com
Yahooligans (Yahoo! for kids) www.yahooligans.com

The search engines **Google** and **Altavista** can also be set to filter out adult content. For encyclopedias and dictionaries, see p.229.

The Angry Beavers
http://members.tripod.com/~foab
A cool fan-site. The official Beaver hangout can be found at:
www.nick.com

Barbie
www.barbie.com
It's a huge, Flash-intensive, slow-loading site, but there's a massive amount of stuff here to keep any girl entertained for hours – so just give in to the inevitable. Your Little Madam might also like to visit:
www.care-bears.com
www.mylittlepony.com

Beakman & Jax
www.bonus.com
Answers to typical kid questions from the likes of "why poo is brown" and "why farts smell" to "why your voice sounds different on a tape recorder" and "why the TV goes crazy while the mixer is on".

The Belch Page
www.goobo.com/belch
Gross out your parents and your little sister.

Bullying Online
www.bullying.co.uk
Advice and support channels for bullied children and their parents.

The Bug Club
www.ex.ac.uk/bugclub
Creepy-crawly fan club with e-pal page, newsletters and pet care sheets on how to keep your newly bottled tarantulas, cockroaches and stick insects alive.

CBeebies
www.bbc.co.uk/cbeebies
This is Auntie's portal for the little 'uns; there are loads of games, stories and things to colour in – a great site. Everyone from *The Fimbles* to *Pingu* gets a look in.

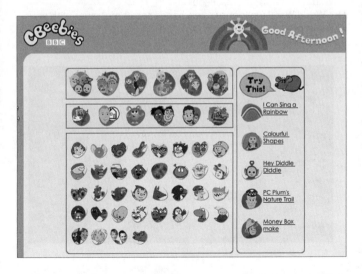

kids & teens

Censored Cartoons
www.toonzone.net/looney/ltcuts
Find out what was removed from your favourite classic cartoon.

Children's Literature Web Guide
www.ucalgary.ca/~dkbrown
Critical round-up of recent kids' books and links to texts.

Club Girl Tech
www.girltech.com
Encourages smart girls to get interested in technology without coming across all geeky.

Cyberteens
www.cyberteens.com
Submit your music, art or writing to a public gallery. You might even win a prize.

Decoding Nazi Secrets
www.pbs.org/wgbh/nova/decoding
Use World War II weaponry to exchange secret messages with your clued-in pals. Also see:
www.thunk.com

Disney.com
www.disney.com
Guided catalogue of Disney's real-world movies, books, theme parks, records, interactive CD-ROMs and such, plus a squeaky-clean Net directory. For an unofficial Disney chaperone, see:
http://laughingplace.com

eHobbies
www.ehobbies.com
Separating junior hobbyists from their pocket money.

Funbrain
www.funbrain.com
Tons of mind-building quizzes, games and puzzles for all ages.

Funschool
www.funschool.com
Educational games for preschoolers.

Goofyface
www.goofyface.com
Gurning from the pros.

Goosebumps
www.tcfhe.com:80/goosebumps/thrillold.html
Scary stories for your next sleepover.

The History Net
www.thehistorynet.com
Bites of world history with an emphasis on the tough guys.

The Idea Box
www.theideabox.com
If your pre-schoolers are bored of The *Fimbles* already, try this site for activities to keep them entertained.

I Used to Believe
http://iusedtobelieve.com
Confess your childhood phobias.

kids & teens

Kids Domain
www.kidsdomain.com
Huge array of stuff here for kids and their parents: brain-builders, games (both online and downloadable), tips on safe surfing, Pokémon, crafts, desktop icons, etc.

Kids Jokes
www.kidsjokes.co.uk
Reams of clean jokes, riddles and knock-knocks.

Kids-Party
www.kids-party.com
Ideas to prevent your child from crying at their own birthday party.

Kids' Space
www.kids-space.org
Hideout for kids to swap art, music and stories with new friends across the world.

Remember these?

Show your kids what you were glued to back in the day ... it's gotta be better than the nonsense they watch now.

Bagpuss www.smallfilms.co.uk/bagpuss
Battle Of The Planets www.akdreamer.com/botp
The Clangers www.clangers.co.uk
The Flumps http://members.lycos.co.uk/theflumps
Hector's House www.davethewave.co.uk/hector/hector.htm
He-Man www.he-man.org/cartoon/cmotu/index.shtml
Ivor The Engine www.smallfilms.co.uk/ivor
Jamie And The Magic Torch www.80snostalgia.com/classictv/jamie
Noggin The Nog www.smallfilms.co.uk/noggin
Pinky & Perky www.pinkyandperky.com
Smurfs www.smurf.com

And for everything else, including *The Littlest Hobo*, *Hear Bear Bunch* and even *Roger Ramjet*, see:

SausageNet www.sausagenet.com

The Little Animals Activity Centre
www.bbc.co.uk/education/laac
The second the music starts and the critters start jiggling you know you're in for a treat. Let your youngest heir loose here after breakfast and expect no mercy until afternoon tea. As cute as it gets.

Magic Tricks
www.magictricks.com
Never believe it's not so. More tricks at:
www.trickshop.com
www.magicweek.co.uk

Neopets
www.neopets.com
Nurture a "virtual pet" until it dies.

Paper Dolls Online
http://collectdolls.about.com/od/paperdolls/
Download 'em, print 'em out, colour 'em in – magic. There are loads of links here to paper dolls, and more still to be had at:
www.paperdollparade.com

Roper's Knots
www.realknots.com
It's not what you know; it's what knots you know.

Secret Languages
www.factmonster.com/ipka/A0769354.html
Learn Double Dutch, Pig Latin and Skimono Jive.

kids & teens

Seussville
www.seussville.com
The online home of the Cat in the Hat, Sam-I-Am, Horton, The Grinch and The Whos.

StarChild
http://starchild.gsfc.nasa.gov
NASA's educational funhouse for junior astronomers. See also:
www.earthsky.com
www.starport.com

Star Wars Origami
www.happymagpie.com/origami.html
Graduate from flapping birds onto Destroyer Droids and Tie Fighters. But, if paper Palpatines ain't your thing, see:
www.aricraft.com.
www.origami.com

Teen Advice
www.teenadvice.net
Part of the enormous Student Center Network, this site has loads of forums and experts for advice on anything from acne to (surprise, surprise) sex. For more advice on tricky subjects, try Embarrassing Problems:
www.embarrassingproblems.co.uk

Toy Stores
www.imaginarium.com
It's just like Christmas all year round. Also see:
www.toysrus.co.uk

The Unnatural Museum
www.unmuseum.org
Lost worlds, dinosaurs, UFOs, pyramids and other mysterious exhibits from the outer bounds of space and time.

Vocabulary
www.vocabulary.co.il
Crosswords, wordsearches, hangman, etc. Great online word games.

What Is Happening to Me?
www.thehormonefactory.com
Find out what's throbbing in your glands.

The Yuckiest Site on the Internet
www.yucky.com
Fun science with a leaning
towards the icky-sticky and
the creepy-crawly. But if
you want to get thoroughly
engrossed in the gross:
www.grossology.org

Law & Crime

For legal primers, lawyer directories, legislation and self-help:

Compact Law www.compactlaw.co.uk
Delia Venables www.venables.co.uk
FindLaw www.findlaw.com
InfoLaw www.infolaw.co.uk
UKLegal www.uklegal.com

For more on criminal activities, trends, arrests and law enforcement, rustle through the following guides:

About Crime http://crime.about.com
Crime Spider www.crimespider.com
Open Directory http://dmoz.org/Society/Crime

A–Z Guide to British Employment Law
www.emplaw.co.uk
Get the upper hand on your boss.

law & crime

The Absolute Worst Things to Say to a Police Officer
www.geocities.com/Heartland/Prairie/7559/copjokes.html
"Aren't you the guy from The Village People?"

Copyright Myths
http://whatiscopyright.org
Just because it's online doesn't make it yours. For even more clarity on the situation, see:
www.templetons.com/brad/copyright.html

The Court Service
www.courtservice.gov.uk
In amongst all the dull information and legalese is a collection of recent judgements handed down by the country's Justices.

Crime Magazine
www.crimemagazine.com
Encyclopedic collection of outlaw tales.

Cybercrime
www.cybercrime.gov
How to report online crooks. More snitching at:
www.cybersnitch.net

Desktop Lawyer
www.desktoplawyer.net
Cut legal costs by doing it online.

Divorce Online
www.divorce-online.co.uk
DIY D.I.V.O.R.C.E. for residents of England and Wales.

Dumb Crooks
www.dumbcrooks.com
Let the masters teach you how not to do it.

Dumb Laws
www.dumblaws.com
Foreign legislation with limited appeal.

ECLS

www.e-commercelawsource.com
Global monitor and directory of online business law.

The Evidence Store

www.evidencestore.com
"Need a hand for your day in court? How about a foot or a skull?...
Accident reconstructions? The Evidence Store's experts will create all
the visual exhibits you'll need to educate even the toughest jury."

FBI Files

http://foia.fbi.gov/alpha.htm
Download the FBI's reports, released by the Freedom of Information
Act, on the Black Panthers, Al Capone, Pablo Picasso, Elvis and
Winston Churchill.

Freelawyer

www.freelawyer.co.uk
Ask a legal question and get a jargon-free response from a qualified
solicitor with a list of local specialists as well as no-obligation esti-
mates.

law & crime

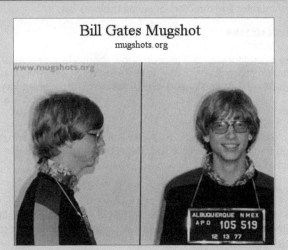

Bill Gates Mugshot
mugshots.org

Lifestyles of the rich and famous. As well as naughty Mr Gates, you'll find the likes of Frank Sinatra, Charles Manson and Steve McQueen:

Famous Mugshots www.mugshots.com
Mugshots.com www.mugshots.com
The Smoking Gun www.thesmokinggun.com/mugshots

Gang Land
www.ganglandnews.com
This amazing site from former New York *Daily News* reporter Jerry Capeci has just about everything you could want to know about Salvatore "Sammy Bull" Gravano, John Gotti, Wing Yeung Chan and their ilk.

Guide to Lock Picking
www.lysator.liu.se/mit-guide/mit-guide.html
Never climb in through the window again.

Legal Services Commission
www.legalservices.gov.uk
Information on Community Legal Service and Criminal Defence
Service from the public body that oversees their administration.

Police Officer's Directory
www.officer.com
Top-of-the-pops cop directory with more than 1500 baddy-nabbing
bureaux snuggled in with law libraries, wanted listings, investigative
tools, hate groups, special ops branches and off-duty homepages.
To see who's in Scotland Yard's bad books:
www.met.police.uk

PursuitWatch
www.pursuitwatch.com
Get paged when there's a live police chase on TV.

Never miss a
High-speed Chase
on Live TV
again!

PursuitAlert™ Alerts you by
phone or pager when a pursuit is
broadcast on live TV.

"Let's cut to the chase..."

Society of Will Writers
www.willwriters.com
Information on wills from the will writers' professional body.

UKSpeedtrap.com
www.ukspeedtraps.co.uk
A great resource for drivers who want to know, umm, where traffic
flashpoints might occur.

maps

Video Vigilante
www.videovigilante.com
If you lived in Oklahoma City, what else would you do but wander the city streets with a video camera looking for guys picking up prostitutes?

Maps

You can generate road and airport maps for most cities world-wide, driving directions for North America and Europe, US traffic reports, world maps and more at:

Expedia http://maps.expedia.com
MapBlast www.mapblast.com
MapQuestUK www.mapquest.co.uk
Easymap www.easymap.co.uk
Mappy www.mappy.co.uk
Multimap www.multimap.com
Ordnance Survey www.ordsvy.gov.uk
Shell Geo Star Route Planner www.shellgeostar.com

For more maps, geographical and GPS resources see:

About http://geography.about.com
Open Directory http://dmoz.org/Reference/Maps

Election-maps.co.uk
www.election-maps.co.uk
Online resource of searchable constituency, county, borough and ward maps. There are loads of tools and fun to be had with map overlays.

Google Maps
http://maps.google.com
It's Google, how could it be anything other than great?

Maps.com
www.maps.com
The world's largest online map retailer; it's based in the US, but has an impressive range of stock, including globes and atlases, and they ship worldwide. For a UK-based alternative, try:
www.elstead.co.uk
www.ordnancesurvey.co.uk
www.stanfords.co.uk

Multimap
www.multimap.com
Probably the best place to start for general map reference – both national and international.

Old-Maps.co.uk
www.old-maps.co.uk
An incredible online database of ancient and historical maps of the British Isles. As if that wasn't enough, you can compare your selections to their modern equivilants and aerial photographs. For even more, and to share your own ancient maps, visit:
www.yourmapsonline.org.uk

StreetMap.co.uk
www.streetmap.co.uk
Very clear and detailed UK maps online; this site always gives fast and reliable search results.

TopoZone
www.topozone.com
For highly detailed US topographic maps, try this site.

Tube Maps
www.tfl.gov.uk/tube/maps
In 1933 Harry Beck designed one of the most famous maps in the world. Check out this site for useful London Underground Tube map resources and some interesting context – don't miss "The Real Underground" link.

Money & Banking

If your bank's on the ball it should offer an online facility to check your balances, pay your bills, transfer funds and export your transaction records into a bean-counting program such as Quicken or Money. If that sounds appealing and your bank isn't already on the case, start looking for a replacement. Go for one you can access via the Internet rather than by dialling direct. That way you can manage your cash through a Web browser whether you're at home, work or in the cybercafé on top of Pik Kommunisma. For help finding a true online bank:

Online Banking Report www.netbanker.com
Qualisteam www.qualisteam.com

If you can resist the urge to day-trade away your inheritance, the Net should give you greater control over your financial future. You can research firms, plot trends, check live quotes, join tip lists and stock forums, track your portfolio live, trade shares and access news. By all means investigate a subscription service or two – at least for the free trial period – but unless you need split-second data feeds or "expert" timing advice you should be able to get by without paying. Start here:

Yahoo! UK http://quote.yahoo.co.uk

Apart from housing the Net's most exhaustive finance directory, **Yahoo!** pillages data from a bunch of the top finance sources and presents it all in a seamless, friendly format. Enter a stock code, for example, and you'll get all the beef from the latest ticker price to a summary of insider trades. In some markets stocks have their own forums, which, let's face it, are only there to spread rumours. In other words, be very sceptical of anything you read or that's sent to you in unsolicited email.

Yahoo! is by no means complete nor necessarily the best in every area, so try a few of these as well:

Bloomberg www.bloomberg.co.uk
CBS MarketWatch http://cbs.marketwatch.com
Digital Look www.digitallook.com
Free Real Time Quotes www.freerealtime.com
Gay Financial Network www.gfn.com
Hemscott www.hemscott.net
Interactive Investor www.iii.co.uk
Microsoft MoneyCentral http://moneycentral.msn.com
Money Extra www.moneyextra.com
Raging Bull www.ragingbull.lycos.com
Sharepages www.sharepages.com

You'll no doubt be after a broker next. As with banking, any broker or fund manager who's not setting up online probably doesn't deserve your business. In fact, many traders are dumping traditional brokers in favour of the exclusively online houses. **E*Trade** (www.etrade.co.uk), for example, offers discount broker-age in at least nine countries (click on "International" to find your local branch). But traditional brokers are catching on. Many have cut their commissions, and offer online services in line with the Internet competition, so it pays to shop around. You might find you prefer to research online and trade by phone. Compare brokers at:

Gomez http://uk.gomez.com

money & banking

For a British e-trading portal, try **E-Trader UK**:

E-Trader UK www.e-traderuk.com

A word of warning, though: some online brokers have experienced outages where they were unable to trade. So if the market crashes in a big way, it mightn't hurt to play safe and use the phone instead.

Advice Online
www.adviceonline.co.uk
Contact an independent financial adviser for help on everything from mortgages to PEP transfers.

Bank of England
www.bankofengland.co.uk
Keep tabs on financial policy decisions.

BigCharts
http://bigcharts.marketwatch.com
Whip up family-sized graphs of US stocks, mutual funds and market indices. More statistical wonders to be had here:
www.livecharts.com
www.citycomment.co.uk
http://stockcharts.com

Banks and building societies

Online banks

Cahoot www.cahoot.com
First Direct (HSBC) www.firstdirect.com
Intelligent Finance www.if.com
Smile (Co-op) www.smile.co.uk
Virgin One Account www.oneaccount.com

▶ account login   bank invest shop why smile? talk to us

welcome to **smile** - the Internet bank

"the best current account in Britain"

High-street banks and building societies – online

Abbey www.abbey.com
Alliance & Leicester www.alliance-leicester.co.uk
Co-operative Bank www.co-operativebank.co.uk
Halifax www.halifax.co.uk
HSBC www.hsbc.co.uk
Lloyds TSB www.lloydstsb.com
Nationwide www.nationwide.co.uk
Natwest www.nwolb.com
Barclays http://ibank.barclays.co.uk

And for a critical look at who's offering the best deals, see:

Find.co.uk www.find.co.uk/Top10/Online_Banks_Top_10

BillPay
www.billpayment.co.uk
Pay your electricity, gas and water bills over the Net with this service
from Alliance & Leicester.

Bonehead Finance
http://ourworld.compuserve.com/homepages/Bonehead_Finance
No-nonsense financial basics for dummies.

money & banking

British Bankers' Association
www.bankfacts.org.uk
Review the Banking Code, find a cash machine, convert currency and consult a glossary of banking terms.

Buy.co.uk
www.buy.co.uk
Tracks and ranks utility prices and finance rates across every UK market. Also links to hundreds of banking sites and investment products. For more rates, try:
www.moneygator.com
www.moneynet.co.uk

Clearstation
http://clearstation.etrade.com
Run your stock picks through a succession of gruelling obstacle courses to weed out the weaklings, or simply copy someone else's portfolio.

Debt Advice
www.debtadvicecentre.co.uk
Get yourself out from the hole.

Earnings Whispers
www.earningswhispers.com
When a stock price falls upon the release of higher-than-expected earnings, chances are that the expectations being "whispered" amongst traders prior to opening were higher than those circulated publicly. Here's where to find out what's being said.

Financial Planning Horizons
www.financial-planning.uk.com
Good, unbiased information on the full range of financial products available in the UK.

Financial Times
www.ft.com
Business news, commentary, delayed quotes and closing prices from London. It's free until you hit the archives.

Tax returns

These days you can do your tax return online – it's easy. For more details and information on obtaining a logon ID, and to get tax information straight from the horse's mouth, go to:

Inland Revenue www.inlandrevenue.gov.uk

To find a qualified adviser, try:

The Chartered Institute of Taxation www.tax.org.uk

For a rough estimate of how much you'll have to pay, try:

UK Wage/Tax Calculator http://listen.to/taxman

For more help and advice with your tax return, as well as links to providers of tax-calculating software, visit:

Advice Guide www.adviceguide.org.uk/em/index/life/tax/tax_returns.htm
QCK www.tax-advice.qck.com
TaxBuddies www.taxbuddies.com

Find
www.find.co.uk
The Financial Information Net Directory houses some 6000 links to UK financial sites, organized into categories such as investment, insurance, information services, advice and dealing, bankings and savings, mortgages and loans, business services and life and pensions.

Foreign Exchange Rates
www.xe.net/ucc
Round-the-clock rates, conversion calculators and intraday charts on pretty close to the full set of currencies. To chart further back, see:
http://pacific.commerce.ubc.ca/xr/plot.html

Frugal Corner
www.frugalcorner.com
Learn how to be thrifty from the experts.

money & banking

FTSE
www.ftse.com
All the data and indices you could ever want.

HedgeWorld
www.hedgeworld.com
Allowing the average Joe a peek inside the secretive world of hedge funds.

Hoovers
www.hoovers.com
Research US, UK and European companies.

iCreditReport
www.icreditreport.com
Dig up any US citizen's credit ratings.

Investment FAQ
www.invest-faq.com
Learn the ropes from old hands.

InvestorWords
www.investorwords.com
Can't tell your hedge rate from your asking price? Brush up on your finance-speak here.

Island
www.island.com
See US equity orders queued up on dealers' screens.

MAXfunds
www.maxfunds.com
Great site that allows you to track the performance of mutual funds. You have to register, but it's free. For more on managed funds and unit trusts, try Standard & Poor's Find Services and TrustNet:
www.funds-sp.com
www.trustnet.com

Missing Money
www.missingmoney.com
Reclaim those US dollars you're owed. More dosh up for grabs here:
www.findcash.com

MoneyChimp
www.moneychimp.com
Plain English primer in the mechanics of financial maths.

MoneyExtra
www.moneyworld.co.uk
Compare financial products and get the best deals.

Money Origami
http://members.cox.net/crandall11/money
It's not how much you earn – it's the way you fold it.

Motley Fool
www.fool.co.uk
Forums, tips, quotes and sound advice. More people telling you
what to do with your money at City Pigeon, Citywire and This Is
Money:
www.citywire.co.uk
www.thisismoney.com

PayPal
www.paypal.com
Arrange online payments through a third party. The payment method of choice for many on eBay.

Pension Sorter
www.pensionsorter.com
Protect yourself against the scandals of the 1980s with this site's
impartial advice. Also check out the Pension Advisory Service, and
for the Government's angle, try Pension Guide or the DWP's site:
www.opas.org.uk
www.pensionguide.gov.uk
www.dwp.gov.uk/lifeevent/penret

Screentrade
www.screentrade.co.uk
General insurance site, offering quotes from a range of insurers. Try also 1st Quote and InsuranceWide:
www.1stquote.co.uk
www.insurancewide.co.uk

Tax & Accounting Sites Directory
www.taxsites.com
Links to everything you need to know about doling out your annual pound of flesh.

UK Insurance Guide
www.ukinsuranceguide.co.uk
Star ratings of nearly all of the UK's insurers.

Wall Street Journal Interactive
www.wsj.com
Not only is this online edition equal to the print one, its charts and data archives give it an edge. That's why you shouldn't complain that it's not free. After all, if it's your type of paper, you should be able to afford it, bigshot.

Museums & Galleries

Homepages of bricks-and-mortar museums:

British Museum www.thebritishmuseum.ac.uk
Guggenheim www.guggenheim.org
The Hermitage www.hermitagemuseum.org
Louvre www.louvre.fr
Metropolitan Museum of Art www.metmuseum.org
Museo Del Prado http://museoprado.mcu.es
Museum of Modern Art www.moma.org
National Gallery www.nationalgallery.org.uk
National Portrait Gallery www.npg.org.uk

Natural History Museum www.nhm.ac.uk
Tate Gallery www.tate.org.uk
Uffizi Gallery www.uffizi.firenze.it
Victoria & Albert Museum www.vam.ac.uk

And if you want to track down a specific artist:

Leonardo da Vinci http://sunsite.dk/cgfa/vinci
Matisse www.ocaiw.com/matisse.htm
Michelangelo www.ibiblio.org/wm/paint/auth/michelangelo
Monet http://webpages.marshall.edu/~smith82/monet.html
Picasso www.tamu.edu/mocl/picasso
Rembrandt www.ibiblio.org/wm/paint/auth/rembrandt
Van Gogh www.vangogh.com

ArtMuseum
www.artmuseum.net
Infrequent exhibitions of modern US classics.

Bitstreams
www.whitney.org/bitstreams
A fine exhibit of minimal digital art from New York's Whitney
Museum, with downloadable art.

museums & galleries

British Lawnmower Museum
www.lawnmowerworld.co.uk
SEE: the world's fastest lawnmower. SEE: Prince Charles's lawnmower.
SEE: the water-cooled egg boiler lawnmower. SEE: Vanessa Feltz's
lawnmower.

Dia Center for the Arts
www.diacenter.org
Web exclusives from "extraordinary" artists, plus the lowdown on the
NY Dia Center's upcoming escapades.

The Exploratorium
www.exploratorium.edu
No substitute for visiting this great San Francisco museum in the
flesh, but the Exploratorium's website is filled with fun and educational sections on sports medicine, the solar system, the Hubble
telescope and the Panama Pacific Exposition.

Isometric Screenshots
http://whitelead.com/jrh/screenshots
An online exhibition by artist Jon Haddock in which he has rendered
some of the twentieth century's defining moments (the protests at
Tiananmen Square, the beating of Rodney King, the assassination of
Martin Luther King) in the visual style of video games.

Museum of Menstruation and Women's Health
www.mum.org
Its curator may be a man, but this is a rather weird and wonderful
site that takes its subject pretty seriously.

Sulabh International Museum of Toilets
www.sulabhtoiletmuseum.org
There goes the neighbourhood.

24 Hour Museum
www.24hourmuseum.org.uk
Portal for British museums, with an excellent search feature which
allows you to look for museums with food, baby changing facilities or that tie-in with national curriculum requirements. Also try

MuseumNetwork or Museums Around the World:
www.museumnetwork.com
www.icom.org/vlmp/world.html
For galleries as well as museums see the Art Guide and The Gallery Channel:
www.artguide.org
www.thegallerychannel.com

Unusual Museums of the Internet

www.unusualmuseums.org
Homepage of the Unusual Museums Webring, your gateway to such exotic destinations as the Toilet Paper Museum, World of Crabs, Cigar Box Art and the Toilet Seat Art Museum.

Web Gallery of Art

www.wga.hu
For fans of everything from Giotto frescoes to Rembrandt's *The Night Watch*, this fantastic site houses digital reproductions of some eight thousand works from between 1150 and 1750.

Web Museum

www.southern.net/wm
Easily one of the best sites on the Web, the Web Museum hosts a fantasy collection of art – like having the Louvre, the Metropolitan Museum of Art, the Hermitage and the Prado all right around the corner. There is also an extensive glossary of terms, artist biographies and enlightening comment on each of the works displayed.

Music

If you're at all into music you've certainly come to the right place. Whether you want to hear it, read about it or watch it being performed you'll be swamped with options. **Artist Direct** should be your first port of call:

Artist Direct www.artistdirect.com

music

Then try these directories:

About.com http://about.com/arts
Open Directory http://dmoz.org/Arts/Music
SonicNet www.sonicnet.com
Yahoo! http://launch.yahoo.com

As ever, if these fail to satisfy, try:

Google www.google.com

For an astoundingly complete music database spanning most popular genres, with bios, reviews, ratings and keyword cross-links to related sounds, sites and online ordering, see:

All Music Guide www.allmusic.com

Much of the mainstream music press is already well established online. You'll find thousands of archived reviews, charts, gig guides, band bios, selected features, shopping links, news, and various sound artefacts courtesy of these familiar beacons:

Billboard www.billboard.com
Dirty Linen www.dirtylinen.com
Folk Roots www.frootsmag.com
Mojo www.mojo4music.com
NME http://nme.com
Q www.q4music.com
Rolling Stone www.rollingstone.com
Vibe www.vibe.com
The Wire www.thewire.co.uk

And if your concentration is up to it, MTV:

Europe www.mtveurope.com
UK www.mtv.co.uk

And if you are after hardware, don't buy a stereo component until you've consulted the world's biggest audio opinion bases:

AudioReview.com www.audioreview.com
AudioWeb www.audioweb.com
What Hi-Fi www.whathifi.com

Or if you wouldn't settle for less than a single-ended triode amp:

Audiophilia www.audiophilia.com
GlassWare www.glass-ware.com
Stereophile www.stereophile.com
Triode Guild www.meta-gizmo.com

Consult these directories for shops and other audio sites:

AudioWorld www.audioworld.com
UK Hi-Fi Dealers http://hifi.dealers.co.uk

Here are a few more of the best music sites to be found online:

Adtunes.com
www.adtunes.com
A one-stop shop for unearthing information about music from commercials, TV shows, video games, etc.

African Music
www.africanmusic.org
World Music buffs should make a beeline for this library, searchable by country or artist, and with an accompanying shopping area.

All About Jazz
www.allaboutjazz.com
Don't let the expensive corporate layout fool you, this American site doesn't just cover Kenny G. As its name suggests, it aims to deal with the entire spectrum of jazz from Anthony Braxton to John Scofield. That it succeeds is down to an easily navigable layout, a wealth of info and contributions from the biggest names in jazz journalism.

Buying records online

Shopping for music is another area where the Net not only equals but outshines its terrestrial counterparts. Apart from the convenience of not having to tramp across town, you can find almost anything on current issue, whether or not it's released locally, and in many cases preview album tracks in RealAudio. You might save money, too, depending on where you buy, whether you're hit with tax and how the freight costs stack up. Consider splitting your order if duty becomes an issue.

The biggest hitch you'll find is when stock is put on back order. Web operators can boast a huge catalogue simply because they order everything on the fly, putting you at the mercy of their distributors. The trouble is your entire order might be held up by one item. The better shops check their stock levels before confirming your order and follow its progress from dispatch to delivery.

As far as where to shop goes, that depends on your taste, but, unless your tastes are very esoteric, you can't go too far wrong with most of the blockbusters:

Amazon www.amazon.co.uk
AudioStreet www.audiostreet.co.uk
BOL www.uk.bol.com
HMV www.hmv.com
101 CD www.101cd.com
Tower Records http://uk.towerrecords.com
Virgin Megastore www.virginmegastores.co.uk

Or, if you're after something more obscure, you'll find no shortage of options under the appropriate **Yahoo!** categories or at:

OffItsFace www.offitsface.com/links.html

You might also want to try one of these:

CDEmusic
www.cdemusic.org
This American site carries not only electronic music from a time when it was made only by men in white lab coats but specialist books, music software and seriously sexy musical equipment such as the Moog Moogerfooger processor.

CD Wow

www.cd-wow.com

Cheap chart CDs (£9 at press time). Also see these German outfits which have enormous catalogues, but are not so cheap:

www.play.com

www.cybercd.de

www.musicexpress.com

Descarga

www.descarga.com

If you are a fan of Latin music, you must, must check out this site. ¡Sabroso!

Dusty Groove

www.dustygroove.com

The website of this renowned Chicago record shop created the blueprint for Internet-based record mail-order services, and they're still doing it better than anyone else. If you're interested in hip-hop, funk, soul, reggae, Latin or obscure soundtracks, it's nearly impossible to leave the site empty-handed.

Forced Exposure

www.forcedexposure.com

This Massachusetts distributor is the colossus of underground music, and its informative, easy-to-use website is another jewel in its crown. Along with an excellent search feature (which, unlike too many mail-order sites, searches the personnel lists as well as the main artist name), the reviews are opinion-ated and informative.

Global Electronic Music Market

http://gemm.com

One-point access to over two million new and used records from almost two thousand sources. See also:

www.secondspin.com

Hard to find records

www.htfr.com

Record-finding agency that specializes in hip-hop, soul and disco vinyl.

Other Music

www.othermusic.com

Since opening in 1996 opposite Tower Records, New York City's bastion of the weird, wacky and just plain great has made a name for itself as one of

music

America's best record emporia. Divided into sections such as "Out" (avant-garde music from this world and others), "In" (1990s indie rock) and "Le Decadanse" (sophisto pop), its site embodies the virtues that made it so good in the first place: friendly, helpful and attitude-free.

Penny Black
www.pennyblackmusic.com
Indie pop, punk and electronica.

Record Finder
www.recordfinders.com
Deleted vinyl, including over 200,000 45s.

Rough Trade
www.roughtrade.com

The website of London's underground landmark is housed in a slick designer package. It would benefit from less time-consuming graphics, but the stock is excellent and the prices, while not the bargain level of the giants, ain't bad. Additional bonuses include an old t-shirt section, chat rooms and downloads – plus there's no tricky spiral staircase to navigate.

Sandbox Automatic
www.sandboxautomatic.com
Without a doubt the best source for independent hip-hop on the Net. There are no bells and whistles, but what a choice.

Secondsounds
www.secondsounds.com
Buying used CDs online may be even more risky than in an actual shop because you can't check out the merchandise, but if you're after a bargain this site is hard to beat.

Sterns African Records Centre
www.sternsmusic.com
The UK's number-one retailer of world music does a fine job online as well.

For a listing of price comparison agents, see Shopping (p.255).

Ari's Simple List of Record Labels
http://recordlabels.nu/index.htm
Exactly what it says on the tin.

Art of the Mixed Tape
www.artofthemix.org
"If you have ever killed an afternoon making a mix, spent the evening making a cover, and then mailed a copy off to a friend after having made a copy for yourself, well, this is the site for you." Kind of says it all, really.

The Bad MIDI Museum
http://littleitaly.fortunecity.com/vatican/791/midi.htm
Not that even "good" MIDI doesn't suck.

Band Family Tree
www.bandfamilytree.com
Secure your place in pop music's genealogy.

B-Boys.com
www.b-boys.com
Hip-hop portal with lots of multimedia content.

The Breaks
www.the-breaks.com
Ever wondered what beat The Beastie Boys ripped off for "Shadrach" or who's sampled Isaac Hayes? This whistle-blowing website tears the lid off the record crates of hip-hop's most famous producers.

music

Classical Music on the Net
www.musdoc.com/classical
Gateway to the timeless.

Classical Net
www.classical.net
An excellent resource for the beginner, with guides to the basic repertoire and building a CD collection. More adventurous listeners may find it a bit wanting, however.

Corporate Anthems – IBM
www.digibarn.com/collections/songs/ibm-songs
What to whistle while you work. There are loads more of these little gems out there – if you find any, please let us know.

The Covers Project
http://covers.wiw.org
The musical version of Six Degrees of Kevin Bacon.

The Dance Music Resource
www.juno.co.uk
New and forthcoming dance releases for mail order, UK radio slots and a stacked directory.

Dancetech
www.dancetech.com
One-stop shop for techno toys and recording tips. For more on synths, try:
www.synthzone.com
www.sonicstate.com

Dave D's Hip-Hop Corner
www.daveyd.com
Hip-hop portal, more at:
www.rapstation.com

Detritus
www.detritus.net
An excellent site devoted to the fringes working on "recycled culture".

Dial-the-Truth Ministries
www.av1611.org
So why does Satan get all the good music?

Dictionaraoke
www.dictionaraoke.org
Hilarious MIDI/Talking Dictionary versions of all your favourite pop hits.

Digizine
www.digidesign.com/digizine
E-zone dedicated to Pro Tools, *the* music editing tool.

Disco-Disco.com
www.disco-disco.com/index.html
Where disco is more than just Afro wigs and flares. More strobe-lit remembrances at:
www.discomusic.com/index.html

DJ University
http://dju.prodj.com
Become a wedding spinner.

The Droplift Project
www.droplift.org
Join in some plunderphonic fun by smuggling some avant-garde sampladelic CDs onto the shelves of major chain retailers.

music

Electronic Musical Instruments
www.obsolete.com/120_years
From the Ondes Martenot to the sampler, this online museum is the liveliest, least techie source of information on the rapidly expanding world of music technology.

Everything Starts With an E
www.everythingstartswithe.co.uk
Sorted old skool rave site with vintage mixes from the early 1990s.

Evil Music
www.evilmusic.com
Don't know the difference between Black Metal and Doom Metal, or what constitutes Original Death Metal as opposed to Brutal Death Metal? Let Spinoza Ray Prozac be your guide to the dark world of the Metal underground.

Fat Lace
www.fatlacemagazine.com
The Internet presence of the hilarious "Magazine for ageing B-boys" contains mostly copy from the print version which covers hip-hop with an irreverent slant only possible in the UK. An added bonus is the Random Old School Name Generator for all the Lord Disco Loves out there.

Freestyling
www.freestyling.com
Fancy yourself as the next Tupac or Jay-Z? Post your best rhyme here and wait to be discovered. For more traditional battling, try Ughh: www.ughh.com

Funk45.com

www.funk45.com

A great entrée into the murky world of deep funk collecting. The site is chock-full of MP3s and RealAudio files of hopelessly obscure funk records. The only catch is that the files are only one minute long, with the aim being to introduce people to this arcane world rather than destroying its informal economy.

Funky Groovy Lexicon

www.funk.ch/funk-lexikon.htm

Over 322 pages (in PDF format), the FGL catalogues nearly everything that can be construed as funky, from 100 Proof Aged in Soul to Zzebra. There's also a gallery of suave cats in dashikis and killer Afros. Believe it or not, it's from Switzerland.

Garage Music

www.garagemusic.co.uk

If you don't live in the East End and want to keep up with what the pirates are playing, click here for the latest news, events and downloads. See also:

www.dubplate.net

Get Out There

www.getoutthere.bt.com

Expose your unsung talents or listen to other unsigned acts. More audition opportunities at:

www.aandronline.com

www.getsigned.com

Gracenote

www.gracenote.com

Automatically supplies track listings for the CDs playing in your PC drive.

Gramophone

www.gramophone.co.uk

There is no better site for serious classical music aficionados. The Web home of *Gramophone* magazine boasts access to its database

music

of 25,000 CD reviews. Need more reasons to visit? How about audio clips, the option to buy from the site, links, listings, glossary, artist bios and feature articles?

Harmony Central
www.harmonycentral.com
Directory and headspace for musicians of all persuasions.

HitSquad
www.hitsquad.com
For software downloads, guitar tabs and loads of other resources for musicians:

Hyperreal
www.hyperreal.org
Perhaps the godfather of all music sites, Hyperreal has been going since 1992. It's a one-stop window shop for all things rave and Ambient. Erowid's Psychoactive Vaults host the raver's version of the *Physician's Desk Reference* – a library of info on mind-altering substances.

Independent Underground Music Archive
www.iuma.com
Full-length tracks and bios from thousands of unsigned and indie-label underground musicians.

Jazz Review
www.jazzreview.com
Bottomless drawer of beard-stroking delights. Also dig:
www.allaboutjazz.com
www.downbeat.com

Kareoke.com
www.kareoke.com
Sing along in the privacy of your own home.

Kompaktkiste
www.kompaktkiste.de
The bluffer's guide to electronic music: an extensive list of CDs of electronic music organized by artist with track listings and running times. It makes no judgements, but if you're looking for that-hard-to-find Phthalocyanine remix, come here first.

Large Hot Pipe Organ
www.lhpo.org
Thrill to the throb of the world's first MIDI-controlled, propane-powered, explosion organ.

Bizarre records

American Song Poem Archives
www.aspma.com
Archive of the bizarre mid-century phenomenon where studio hacks set music to the lyrics of ordinary Joes – resulting in some of the weirdest records ever.

Frank's Vinyl Museum
http://franklarosa.com/$spindb.query.new.vinyl
Exhibition of charity-shop flotsam, including such classics as Ken Demko Live at the Lamplighter Inn and an LP of Beatles covers done by dogs.

The Internet Museum of Flexi/Cardboard/Oddities
www.wfmu.org/MACrec
Records made out of metal, souvenirs from the Empire State Building and other curios.

Songs in the Key of Z
www.keyofz.com/keyofz
Irwin Chusid's fantastic introduction to the world of outsider music. More at: www.incorrectmusic.com

music

Last FM
www.last.fm
Online music station where you create your own personalized music page and get hooked up to others with similar tastes.

Launch.com
http://launch.yahoo.com
Thousands of music videos, audio channels, reviews and forums.

London Musicians Collective
www.l-m-c.org.uk
The LMC has been promoting the cause of improvised music in the Big Smoke for over a quarter of a century. Their site features content from their journal, *Resonance*, streaming audio from their radio show and information on studio facilities.

Lyrics Search Engine
http://lyrics.astraweb.com
Finding song lyrics on the Web is a science constantly fraught with difficulty due to copyright laws, but for now this site reigns. See also: www.thesonglyrics.com

The Manual
www.klf.de/online/books/bytheklf/manual.htm
Fancy trying pop superstardom? Have a glance at the essential guide to superstardom, written by the ace pranksters in The KLF.

Metal Sudge
www.metal-sludge.com
Heavy metal portal that treats the genre with the dignity and respect it deserves.

MIDI Farm
www.midifarm.com
Synthesized debasements of pop tunes, TV themes and film scores.

Mr Lucky
www.mrlucky.com
Get smooth with rhythm 'n' booze.

Niceup
www.niceup.com
Probably the most irie reggae site on the Net, Niceup contains discographies, articles on topics like "Studio One Riddims", a lyrics archive, histories, news and a patois dictionary.

Online Guitar Archive
www.olga.net
A truly awesome site for guitarists and bassists. No more scurrying through back issues of *Guitar Player* for tablature for Blue Öyster Cult's "Godzilla" – OLGA boasts some 40,000 tabs.

Original Hip Hop Lyrics Archive
www.ohhla.com
Mind-blowingly complete archive of all of your favourite rhymes.

Perfect Sound Forever
www.furious.com/perfect
Calling itself "the online magazine with the warped attitudes", PSF is one of the best music sites on the Net. Although most of the articles are straight interviews and don't take advantage of the Web format, the writing on left-field heroes is passionate and informative.

music

MP3s

Unlike every music delivery system since the development of 331/3 and 45 rpm records, the MP3 format was not forced upon consumers by the record industry. Short for "MPEG-1 audio layer 3", MP3 is a file format that allows compression of recorded music without a significant degradation in sound quality, and it has become the standard way of storing music on the Internet. In order to make the most of MP3 you need a PC or Mac with at least 32MB of RAM, a 56K modem, lots of room on your hard drive and, if you have an older machine, you might have to install a sound card. You will also need some MP3 player software such as **Soundjam** for a Mac or **Winamp** or **RealJukebox** for PC, though you will probably find that your computer can already handle the files using built-in tools such as **Windows Media Player** or Apple's **iTunes** on a Mac. For more on software, see **MP3.com**, which as well as lots of music has links to all the downloadable MP3 players and lots of information for beginners:

MP3.com www.mp3.com

You shouldn't have any trouble finding MP3 music online, though not everything you'll find is legal. The legal side consists mainly of pay-to-download tracks and free previews authorized by the record label. These tend to be from acts that can't get airplay and are eager for exposure, but that's not necessarily the case. As for pay-to-download, try these sites for legal MP3s:

All of MP3 www.allofmp3.com
Artist Direct www.artistdirect.com
AudioGalaxy www.audiogalaxy.com
ClickMusic www.clickmusic.co.uk
Dmusic www.dmusic.com
eClassical www.eclassical.com
Epitonic www.epitonic.com
IUMA www.iuma.com
Launch.com www.launch.com
Liquid Audio www.liquid.com
Listen.com www.listen.com
Peoplesound www.peoplesound.com

There are also subscription services that provide a certain number of downloads (usually combined with lots of lo-fi streams) for a monthly fee. For example:

MusicNet www.musicnet.com
Pressplay www.pressplay.com
Rhapsody www.listen.com

So what about the illegal side? Basically, many programs allow computer users to "rip" music – convert a track on a CD into an MP3 file. Once that's done, they can distribute their files around the world – and download other people's – without any record company mediation.

Most illegal MP3s are exchanged not via the Web but via peer-to-peer file-sharing networks. These aren't illegal in themselves, but they are mostly used to share music (plus software and film) illegally without the copyright holder's consent. To connect to a network and search for files, a user simply needs an appropriate program for that network. The biggest networks are accessible with:

Emule www.emule-project.net
KaZaA Lite www.kazaalite.com
WinMX www.winmx.com

Some file-sharers claim that their activities will ultimately benefit musicians by removing the corporate domination of an art form. Naturally, the record industry – led by the Record Industry Association of America – is unconvinced and has tried to put a stop to free file exchanges. And it's not just pop stars and big business that are complaining. Independent musicians, too, are worried about their royalties. Read various points of view at:

Coalition for the Future of Music www.futureofmusic.org
Free Music Philosophy www.ram.org/ramblings/philosophy/fmp.html
RIAA www.riaa.com

Finally, there's the Apple Music Store, an online music download site which can be accessed only by using Apple's iTunes software. Once you have the program you can register your payment details with the store and start browsing the music and eBooks on offer directly from iTunes. For the full story pick up a copy of *The Rough Guide to iPods, iTunes & Music Online*.

The Apple Music Store www.apple.com/itunes/store

music

Pitchfork Media
www.pitchforkmedia.com
Indie news, reviews and features and more.

Rap Dictionary
www.rapdict.org
Can't understand your teenage son anymore? Log on here, dun, and you'll get the 411.

Roadie.net
www.roadie.net
No backstage pass necessary.

Rocklist
www.rocklist.co.uk
Quarter of a decade's worth of best-of-the-year lists from the top mags.

Scratch Simulator
www.turntables.de
Can't afford a pair of SL 1200s? Practise your reverse orbit scratches and beat juggling here, or at Infinite Wheel:
www.infinitewheel.com

Shareware Music Machine
www.hitsquad.com/smm
Tons of shareware music players, editors and composition tools, for every platform.

Sheet Music Archive
www.sheetmusicarchive.net
A great resource of copyright-free downloadable sheet music. You can download only two scores each day – but that shouldn't be a problem, unless you are a very fast learner.

Show and Tell Music
www.showandtellmusic.com
Albums much cooler than anything you own.

Smithsonian Institution
www.si.edu
Although this site is as gigantic as the famous American museum itself, if you're interested in folk music (from both America and the rest of the world) it's an absolute paradise, with info on their Folkways record label, webcasts, galleries and articles (augmented with RealAudio files).

Songplayer
www.songplayer.com
Can't read music and still want to play guitar like Hendrix or keyboards like Keith Emerson? Try this music tuition site which has some four thousand songs in its files, and there are no cumbersome staves, bars or clefs to wrestle with.

Sonic Net
www.sonicnet.com
Big-name live cybercasts, streaming video channels, chats, news and reviews.

Sony
www.sony.com
Think about everything that Sony flogs. Now imagine it all squeezed under one roof.

welcome to the
world of **Sony**
music, movies, TV, games, electronics

Soul City
www.soulcity.ndo.co.uk
Listen to hundreds of 1960s and Northern Soul clips.

music

Soulman's World of Beats

www.worldofbeats.com/old_site

E-zine for all the crate diggers, with articles focusing on the samples from all of your favourite hip-hop records. More vinyl obsession at:

www.breakz4dayz.com

www.samplehead.com

Sounds Online

www.soundsonline.com

Preview loops and samples, free in RealAudio. Pay to download studio quality. If it's effects you're after, try:

www.sounddogs.com

Taxi

www.taxi.com

Online music A&R service. And guess what? You and your plastic kazoo are just what they're looking for.

Theremin Resources

www.thereminworld.com

All the history of those "Good Vibrations", and a whole lot more. To build your own, see:

http://home.att.net/~theremin1

This Day in Music
www.thisdayinmusic.com
Find out which member of The Bay City Rollers shares your birthday, and other essential music trivia.

Urban Sounds
www.urbansounds.com
Excellent, well-planned and designed electronica site from the US. The Minimalism issue features hot names on the underground and is sexily intercut with Rem Koolhaas sketches and Donald Judd reproductions.

WholeNote
www.wholenote.com
Guitar resources and chat boards. For live lessons, see:
www.riffinteractive.com

Nature

3D Insects
www.ento.vt.edu/~sharov/3d/3dinsect.html
Whizz around a selection of 3D bugs. They're not real insects but at least they don't have pins through their backs. Also see what's creeping and crawling at:
http://insects.org

African Wildlife Foundation
www.awf.org
Great site covering everything from the aardvark to the zebra.

Animal Diversity Web
http://animaldiversity.ummz.umich.edu
Database of animal history, classification, distribution and conservation from the University of Michigan. More at Natureserve:
www.natureserve.org

nature

Aquatic Network
www.aquanet.com
A good site promoting sustainable aquaculture, with some great photography and solid information saving it from being too earnest.

ARKive
www.arkive.org
Electronic archive of the world's endangered species.

Birding
http://birding.about.com
Birds are such regional critters that one site couldn't hope to cover them all. Use this page to find the chirpiest one on your block. More fine feathered friends listed at:
www.camacdonald.com/birding
http://dmoz.org/Recreation/Birding

Birds of Britain
www.birdsofbritain.co.uk
Webzine devoted to our fine feathered friends, with an illustrated guide of around a hundred species.

Cetacea.org
www.cetacea.org
Excellent encyclopedic source of information on whales, dolphins and porpoises.

Dinosaur Interplanetary Gazette
www.dinosaur.org
It may be as slow and cumbersome as a brontosaurus stuck in the LaBrea tar pits, but patience does pay off with a wealth of information and features.

The Electronic Zoo
http://netvet.wustl.edu/e-zoo.htm
Up and running since 1993, this virtual menagerie is the best collection of animal-related links on the Web.

EMBL Reptile Database

www.embl-heidelberg.de/~uetz/LivingReptiles.html

Slither through for info on everything from turtles to amphisbaenae.

eNature.com

www.enature.com

Vibrant field guides to North American flora and fauna.

Field Trips

www.field-guides.com/vft/index.htm

A neat idea, if not perfectly executed: visit this site and take virtual field trips involving deserts, oceans, hurricanes, sharks, fierce creatures, salt marshes, volcanoes and other natural wonders.

Forces of Nature

http://library.thinkquest.org/C003603

Thinkquest's student-designed website devoted to avalanches, droughts, landslides, earthquakes and other natural disasters.

ForestWorld

www.forestworld.com

Timber tales from both sides of the 'dozer. Also check out: http://forests.org

nature

Great Cats of the World
www.greatcatsoftheworld.com
The homepage of the Bridgeport Nature Center in Texas functions as
a mini-encyclopedia of lions, tigers, leopards and cougars.

Insects on the Web
www.insects.org
Definitely not one for your little girl, this excellent educational
resource of creepy-crawlies features some rather too detailed photography of everyone's least favourite bugs.

Nessie on the Net
www.lochness.co.uk
Watch the Loch Ness webcam, spot the monster and win £1000.

Predator Urines
www.predatorpee.com
Bewitch neighbouring Jack Russells with a dab of bobcat balm or
true blue roo poo:
www.roopooco.com

Sea turtle migration-tracking
www.cccturtle.org/satwelc.htm
Adopt a bugged sea reptile and follow its trail.

World Wildlife Fund
www.wwf.org.uk
Teach your kids that the WWF isn't all about pile drivers and steroid
cases in skimpy shorts. More animal lovers at the World Society for
the Protection of Animals and the Royal Society for the Protection of
Animals:
www.wspa.org.uk
www.rspca.org.uk

News, Newspapers & Magazines

Now that almost every magazine and newspaper on the globe from *Ringing World* (www.ringingworld.co.uk) to the *Falkland Island News* (www.sartma.com) is discharging daily content onto the Net, it's beyond this guide to do much more than list a few of the notables and then point you in the right direction for more. The simplest way to find your favourite read would be to look for its address in a recent issue. Failing that, try entering its name into a subject guide or search engine. If you don't have a title name and would prefer to browse by subject or region, try:

Open Directory http://dmoz.org/News
Yahoo! http://dir.yahoo.com/News_and_Media

Some newspapers replicate themselves word for word online, but most provide enough for you to live without giving you the complete paper edition. Still, that's not bad considering they're generally free online before the paper even hits the stands. Apart from whatever proportion of their print they choose to put online, they also tend to delve deeper into their less newsy areas such as travel, IT, entertainment and culture. Plus they often bolster this with exclusive content such as breaking news, live sports coverage, online shopping, opinion polls and discussion groups. There are also a few sites that index multiple news archives, though usually at a price. Such as:

Electric Library www.elibrary.com
FindArticles.com www.findarticles.com
NewsLibrary www.newslibrary.com
Northern Light www.nlsearch.com

news, newspapers & magazines

All of the popular news bugles have a presence online, most with an address that you shouldn't have too much trouble figuring out (www.guardian.co.uk, www.thesun.co.uk, etc). If there are any that you can't find, try **Google** or see if the address is printed somewhere on the paper version.

Like much you do online, reading news is addictive. You'll know you're hooked when you find yourself checking into newswires throughout the day to monitor moving stories. Try these for breaking news:

Ananova www.ananova.com
Associated Press www.ap.org
BBC http://news.bbc.co.uk
CNN www.cnn.com
ITN www.itn.co.uk
NBC www.msnbc.msn.com
Reuters www.reuters.com
Sky www.sky.com
Wired News www.wired.com

Or perhaps best of all, use a free news aggregator, which taps into several sources simultaneously. These ones are good for UK content:

Google News UK http://news.google.co.uk
NewsNow www.newsnow.co.uk
Yahoo! News UK http://uk.news.yahoo.com

News tickers

News tickers place a thin ticker-tape-like strip along the top or bottom of the Desktop or sometimes a floating panel, which, depending on the ticker you have, displays a continuous trickle of headlines, share prices, weather reports, etc. More often than not they are downloadable from, and updated by, one particular site, such as the BBC's, but there are also news aggregating tickers available which draw from multiple news sources. They work best with an always-on connection, but the best very thing about these little utilities is that they are free.

BBC Newsline www.bbc.co.uk/newsline
CoolTick (stock ticker) www.cooltick.com
Desktop News www.desktopnews.com
Weather tickers http://weather.about.com/cs/weathertools
WorldFlash www.worldflash.com

But there's plenty more at:

Arts & Letters Daily www.aldaily.com
Asia Observer www.asiaobserver.com
NewsHub www.newshub.com
Russian Story www.russianstory.com
TotalNews www.totalnews.com

If you want to search news blogs (see p.201), probably the best way is to use:

DayPop www.daypop.com

To find more specialist publications, you may want to try a directory of newspapers and news organizations on the Web, which will help you track down everything from Bulgarian National Radio to Zambian broadsheets.

NewsLink http://newslink.org
Editor & Publisher www.editorandpublisher.com

news, newspapers & magazines

Metagrid www.metagrid.com
NewsDirectory www.newsdirectory.com
Online Newspapers www.onlinenewspapers.com

As for magazines, most maintain a site but they're typically more of an adjunct to the print than a substitute. Still, some are worth checking out, especially if they archive features and reviews or break news between issues. Again, check a recent issue for an address, or a directory such as:

The Magazine Boy www.themagazineboy.com

And as you might expect, there's no shortage of tech news out there on the Web:

iSUBSCRIBE www.isubscribe.co.uk
NewsLinx www.newslinx.com
SiliconValley www.siliconvalley.com
Tech News www.news.com
TechWeb www.techweb.com
ZD Network News www.zdnet.com

And if you want e-business news:

InternetNews www.internetnews.com

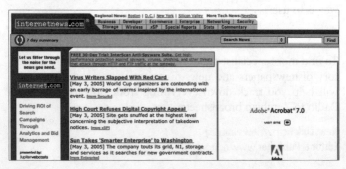

E-zines

"E-zines" are magazines that exist only online or are delivered by email. But because almost any regularly updated webpage or blog fits this description, the term has lost much of its currency. Although most e-zines burn out as quickly as they appear, a few of the pioneers are still kicking on. For more, try browsing a directory at:

www.ezine-dir.com
http://zinos.com

ABC All 'Bout Computers http://personal-computer-tutor.com/abc
Loads of handy PC tips, tricks and advice.

Drudge Report www.drudgereport.com
The shock bulletin that set off the Lewinsky avalanche. A one-hit wonder perhaps, but still a bona fide tourist attraction on the info goat track.

Future File http://futurefile.com
Thought-provoking e-zine portal from technocrat Todd Maffin, featuring ideas and trends to look for in the next decade.

Gurl.com www.gurl.com
Zine dedicated to hip young things pitched somewhere between the original Sassy and Jane.

IGN www.ign.com/affiliates/index.html
The Internet Gaming Network treads similar – though generally tamer – ground to UGO, partnering mostly with high-quality gaming, sci-fi, wrestling and comic sites.

The Register www.theregister.com
The best source for daily tech news straight to your inbox.

Spiked www.spiked-online.com
Caustic, political e-zine from former *Living Marxism* supremo Mick Hume.

Suck www.suck.com
Arguably the only e-zine that ever mattered. Its archives are still worth reading, if not for its cocked eye on all that's wired and painfully modern then at least for Terry Colon's cartoons.

Underground Online www.ugo.com
Big men's magazine-style network devoted to music, wrestling, film, TV, books, technology and so on.

news, newspapers & magazines

AlterNet

www.alternet.org

Roundup of almost all of America's alternative weekly papers.

American Newspeak

www.scn.org/news/newspeak

Celebrating the arts of doublethink, spin, media coaching and other ways to mangle meaning.

Crayon

www.crayon.net

Most of the major portals such as Excite, Yahoo! and MSN also allow you to create a custom news page that draws from several sources – though none does it quite so thoroughly as Crayon. Infobeat does similar things but delivers by email:

www.infobeat.com

DavesDaily

www.davesdaily.com

A compendium of the weirdest news and views from around the world.

A Journalist's Guide to the Internet

http://reporter.umd.edu

No design whatsoever, but a useful set of links to resources for journalists. More for hacks at:

www.journaliststoolbox.com

www.cyberjournalist.net

http://mediapoint.press.net

MediaLens

www.medialens.org

Suspicious of our beloved "free" press? You will be once you've visited this site.

Moreover

www.moreover.com

The best free service for searching current or recent stories across hundreds of international news sources. Also try News Index and

What the Papers Say:
www.newsindex.com
www.whatthepaperssay.co.uk
Like someone to monitor the Web and assorted newswires for mention of your product or misdeeds? Try:
www.webclipping.com

MyVillage
www.myvillage.com
Online community with an emphasis on local news. Best in and around London, but slowly increasing their profile across the country.

The Onion
www.theonion.com
News the way it was meant to be.

This Is True
www.thisistrue.com
Randy Cassingham's weekly column of preposterous-but-true news stories and headlines, collated from the major wire services.

Wireless Flash News Service
www.flashnews.com
News service specializing in pop culture stories, featuring some of the least newsworthy headlines in history.

World Press Review
www.worldpress.org
Keeping tabs on the people who keep tabs on us. Also keep an eye on News Watch:
www.newswatch.org

RSS newsfeeds

These days most news websites and blogs – and lots of other sites as well – offer "newsfeeds" based on Really Simple Syndication (RSS). Each feed consists of a series of headlines that link to a story on the site. The beauty of the system is that you can see at a glance what's new without actually having to visit the site. Browsers such as Firefox have RSS capability built in, allowing you to see the headlines at a news site directly from your bookmarks bar (see picture). Or you could use a standalone newsreader, or "aggregator", such as SharpReader (Windows) or NetNews Wire (Mac) to keep an eye on lots of sites simultaneously.

SharpReader (Windows) www.sharpreader.net
NetNews Wire (Mac) http://ranchero.com/netnewswire

Outdoor Pursuits

Birdlinks
www.birdlinks.co.uk
Gateway to the world of birdwatching. More to look at on:
http://birding.about.com
www.camacdonald.com/birding
http://dmoz.org/Recreation/Birding
www.birdsofbritain.co.uk

The Butterfly Website
www.butterflywebsite.com
The Monarch of butterfly sites, with galleries, lists of gardens and butterfly gardens and loads of information on biology, conservation and behaviour.

Camp Sites
www.camp-sites.co.uk
Find a place to pitch in the UK. More nights under canvas here:
www.campinguk.com

Go Fishing
www.go-fishing.co.uk
Your complete angling resource. Other sites that would make Isaak Walton proud:
www.anglersnet.co.uk
www.angling-news.co.uk

Great Outdoor Recreation Pages
www.gorp.com
Ignore all the multivitamin and SUV adverts and the American bias because this is the best outdoors site on the Web. The superlative how-to pages alone make it worth navigating the pop-up ads.

Ramblers' Association
www.ramblers.org.uk
All the latest news on walking and other pedestrian pursuits. For more info, take your browser on a stroll over to Walking World or Walking Britain:
www.walkingworld.com
www.walkingbritain.co.uk

Rock Climbing in the UK
www.ukcrags.com
Great resource for British rock climbers, with news, articles, web-cams, events listings, routes and crag descriptions. More handholds can be found at Climb Guide and Bouldering.com:
www.climb-guide.com
www.bouldering.com

Pets

About Veterinary Medicine

http://vetmedicine.about.com

About's vet pages are an excellent resource for pet owners worried about their moggie or pet lizard and are filled with advice, news, disease indexes and forums.

The Aviary

www.theaviary.com/ci.shtml

Everything you'd ever want to know about companion birds – and then some.

Barbara's Canine Café

www.k9treat.com

Only In America part 346: If your mutt's got a food allergy or you just want to get your hound a "celebration gift basket" made from all-natural ingredients, look no further.

Chazhound
www.chazhound.com
Resources for dog lovers as well as screensavers, games and doggie greetings cards.

The Dogpatch
www.dogpatch.org
Advice on training your pooch, plus the best canine links on the Web.

Dogs
www.dogs.co.uk
Pages for British dog owners, including loads of links to dog-friendly accommodation.

Equine World
www.equine-world.co.uk
Great site covering all things equestrian. See also Equiworld: www.equiworld.net

FishDoc
www.fishdoc.co.uk
All the information you need if your goldfish is looking a bit green around the gills. For aquarium links go to: www.fishlinkcentral.com

House Rabbit Society
www.rabbit.org
Online community and resource for rabbit owners. Also try: www.rabbitwelfare.co.uk/index.htm

Kingsnake.com
www.kingsnake.com
A mind-bogglingly enormous portal for reptile and amphibian enthusiasts.

pets

Moggies
www.moggies.co.uk
In addition to the usual information and advice, this feline resource allows you to create a virtual cat and even offers horoscopes for Tiddles. Also, visit Frank the cat at:
www.cathospital.co.uk

Mr Winkle
www.mrwinkle.com
Ok, so how cute is Mr Winkle? But is he really real?

Museum of Non-Primate Art
www.monpa.com
Online home of the people behind the "Why cats paint" caper, with special exhibitions devoted to dancing with cats and "bird art".

New Pet.com
www.newpet.com
Friendly and informative site for new or soon-to-be owners of a cat or dog.

Pet Mad
www.petmad.com
Despite first appearances, this Irish site is probably the best (and cheapest) online pet shop for UK surfers.

Pet Planet
www.petplanet.co.uk
Not to be confused with the American site listed below, this site houses one of the UK's best online pet shops, with special features like a lost pet service and rehoming facilities.

The Pet Project
www.thepetproject.com
There's a whiff of New Age aromatherapy here ("the special bond between human and animal") and the focus is firmly on the US, but this is surely the most comprehensive pet resource on the Web, with all manner of advice on everything from canine nutrition to interpreting the sounds your chinchilla makes.

Rodent Fancy
www.rodentfancy.com
With information on everything from African rock rats to Mongolian gerbils, rodent fanciers shouldn't look anywhere else.

RSPCA Online
www.rspca.org.uk
The RSPCA's homepage offers advice, allows the kids to adopt a cyber-pet before getting the real thing and features news and information on campaigns for animal welfare.

Save Toby
www.savetoby.com
At the time of going to press, the owner of Toby the rabbit has claimed that he will eat his fluffy friend if he doesn't receive $50,000 of online donations. By the time you read this Toby may be little more than a tasty memory, but it'll still be worth checking out the site's "hate mail" page.

Photography

American Museum of Photography
www.photographymuseum.com
Exhibitions from back when cameras were a novelty.

Black & White World
www.photogs.com/bwworld
A celebration of black-and-white photography.

British Journal of Photography
www.bjphoto.co.uk
Homepage of the venerable magazine and a valuable resource for
the professional photographer.

Digital Camera Resource Page
www.dcresource.com
A simple, easy-to-use site, offering reviews of loads of digital cameras
and equipment as well as product news and information on issues
like Mac OS X compatibility.

Digital Photography Review
www.dpreview.com
Considering a new digital camera? Read on.

Digital Truth: Photo Resource
www.digitaltruth.com
Perhaps the best photographic resource for the advanced photographer, with loads of tips, downloadable f-stop calculation software and "the world's largest" film development chart.

Exposure
www.88.com/exposure
A beginner's guide to photography, whose neatest feature is the simulated camera which mimics the effects of adjustments in shutter speed and aperture on pictures.

Invisible Light
www.atsf.co.uk/ilight/photos/index.html
Your complete guide to infrared photography.

Life
www.lifemag.com
View *Life* magazine's Picture of the Day, then link through to some of the world's most arresting photographs. There's even more over at *Time*'s Picture Collection and Australia's Newsphotos:
www.thepicturecollection.com
www.newsphotos.com.au

photography

Got some snaps you'd like to show the world – or just your friends (through selective password access)? Upload them here:

Album Pictures www.albumpictures.com
Club Photo www.clubphoto.com
MSN Photos http://photos.msn.com/home.aspx
Photobox www.photobox.co.uk
PhotoLoft www.photoloft.com
Picture Trail www.picturetrail.com
Web Shots www.webshots.com
Yahoo! Photos http://photos.yahoo.com

Masters of Photography
www.masters-of-photography.com
An excellent collection of the works of some of history's greatest snappers, from Berenice Abbott to Garry Winogrand. In addition to the images, there are links to articles and other websites with biographical and technical information.

Photodisc
http://creative.gettyimages.com/photodisc
Plunder these photos free, or pay for the hi-res versions.

PhotoWave
www.photowave.com
Portal for professional photographers. Amateurs should try:
www.photo.net
www.photolinks.net
www.stilljournal.com
http://photography.about.com

PhotoZone
www.photozone.de
This site offers comparative analysis of cameras and lenses, and loads of technical information on all sorts of equipment.

Pinhole Visions
www.pinhole.com
A great site devoted to the art of pinhole photography, a primitive form of picture-taking that creates a dreamlike effect unattainable with conventional photography. There are two gallery spaces, discussion groups, news and links to other resources.

Shutterbug
www.shutterbug.net
The online home of the American *Shutterbug* magazine includes a massive archive of past articles, product reviews, news, hints, galleries, competitions and more. Digital photographers should focus on eDigital Photo:
www.edigitalphoto.com

Take Better Photos
http://betterphotos.cjb.net
No-nonsense site offering tricks and tips on correcting common photographic errors, picking the best viewpoint, compensating for parallax, computer enhancement, etc, etc. For more serious (really serious) tuition at a cost, try Photo Seminars:
www.photo-seminars.com

Year in the Life of Photojournalism
www.digitalstoryteller.com/YITL
Tag along with pros and see what they do day to day.

Politics & Government

Most governmental departments, politicians, political aspirants and causes maintain websites to spread the word and further their various interests. To find your local rep or candidate, start at their party's homepage. These typically lie dormant unless there's a campaign in progress, but can still be a good source of contacts to badger. Government departments, on the other hand, tirelessly belch out all sorts of trivia right down to transcripts of minis-

politics & government

terial radio interviews. So if you'd like to know about impending legislation, tax rulings, budget details and so forth, skip the party pages and go straight to the department. If you can't find its address through what's listed below, try:

Yahoo! http://dir.yahoo.com/Government
Open Directory http://dmoz.org/Society/Government

For the latest election night counts, check the breaking news sites (p.198). Below is a selection of the most useful starting points.

British Politics Links www.ukpol.co.uk
Green Party www.greenparty.org.uk
Labour www.labour.org.uk
Liberal Democrats www.libdems.org.uk
National Assembly for Wales www.wales.gov.uk
Natural Law www.natural-law-party.org.uk
Northern Ireland Assembly www.niassembly.gov.uk
Plaid Cymru www.plaidcymru.org
Prime Minister www.pm.gov.uk
Scottish National Party www.snp.org
Scottish Parliament www.scottish.parliament.uk
Sinn Féin www.sinnfein.ie
Social Democratic and Labour Party www.sdlp.ie
Socialist Party www.socialistparty.org.uk
Socialist Workers Party www.swp.org.uk
Tories www.conservatives.com
Ulster Unionist Party www.uup.org

Adopt-A-Minefield
www.adoptaminefield.com
Help clear war-torn communities of deadly explosives.

Amnesty International
www.amnesty.org
Join the battle against brutal regimes and injustice.

Antiwar
www.antiwar.com
Challenges US intervention in foreign affairs, especially in the Balkans and Middle East.

The Big Breach
www.thebigbreach.com
Download a free copy of the British MI6 spy-and-tell book.

Bilderberg Group
www.bilderberg.org
Read about the people who really rule the world.

The British Monarchy
www.royal.gov.uk
Tune into the world's best-loved soap opera.

British Politics Pages
www.ukpolitics.org.uk
News and history for politicos, with a great links page.

Center for the Moral Defense of Capitalism
www.moraldefense.com
Is greed still good in the Y2Ks? Maybe not good but legal, says Microsoft's last bastion of sympathy. Also see:
www.aynrand.org

politics & government

Central Intelligence Agency
www.cia.gov
Want the inside story on political assassinations, arms deals, Colombian drug trades, spy satellites, phone tapping, covert operations, government-sponsored alien sex cults and the X-files? Well, guess what? Never mind, you won't go home without a prize – see: www.copvcia.com

Communist Internet List
www.cominternet.org
Angry intellectuals and workers unite. Also visit:
www.yclusa.org

The Complete Bushisms
http://slate.msn.com/default.aspx?id=76886
The subliminable wit and wisdom of George Dubya.

Conspiracies
www.mt.net/~watcher
www.conspire.com
Certain people are up to something and, what's worse, they're probably all in it together. Click here for the biggest cover-ups of all time.

DirectGov
www.direct.gov.uk
Not to be confused with the ISP, this UK Online aims to be the place where people interact with the Government. Like most governmental policies, it seems pretty hazy and to get anywhere you have to dig far too hard.

Disinformation
www.disinfo.com
The dark side of politics, religious fervour, new science, along with current affairs you won't find in the papers.

Political blogs

As you might expect, some of the best blogs to be found online are politically charged. Browse the eTalking directory to find your political allies:

eTalkinghead http://directory/etalkinghead.com

Some of the most interesting political blogs are those written by MPs and councillors, honestly:

Richard Allan http://richardallan.org.uk (Lib Dem)
Paul Cumming www.paulcumming.blogspot.com (Conservative)
Austin Mitchell www.austinmitchell.org (Labour)
Tom Watson www.tom-watson.co.uk (Labour)

For further commentary and insight, try:

Paul Anderson http://libsoc.blogspot.com
Bloggerheads www.bloggerheads.com/politicians.asp
British Politics http://britishspin.blogspot.com

Doonesbury

www.doonesbury.com
Over thirty years of Gary Trudeau's legendary political cartoon.

Electronic Frontier Foundation

www.eff.org
Protecting freedom of expression on the Internet.

ePolitix

www.epolitix.com
British politics portal.

Fax Your MP

www.faxyourmp.com
Pester your local member through an Internet-to-fax gateway.

FBI FOIA Reading Room

http://foia.fbi.gov
FBI documents released as part of the Freedom of Information Act.

politics & government

Includes a few files on such celebrities as John Wayne, Elvis, Marilyn and the British Royals. Check out who's most wanted now at:
www.fbi.gov

Federation of American Scientists
www.fas.org
Heavyweight analysis of science, technology and public policy including national security, nuclear weapons, arms sales, biological hazards, secrecy and space policy.

Foreign Report
www.foreignreport.com
Compact subscription newsletter with a track record of predicting international flashpoints well before the dailies.

Free Tibet
www.freetibet.org
Favourite website of The Beastie Boys and Richard Gere.

Freedom Forum
www.freedomforum.org
Organization dedicated to free-speech issues, newsroom diversity and freedom of the press.

The Gallup Organization
www.gallup.com
Keep track of opinion trends and ratings.

Gates Foundation
www.gatesfoundation.org
See where the world's second richest man is spreading it around.

Gay & Lesbian Alliance against Defamation
www.glaad.org
Stand up against media stereotyping and discrimination against those deviating from the heterosexual norm. For more news, advice and dispatches from the activist front, try:
www.stonewall.org.uk
www.actupny.org

Gendercide
www.gendercide.org
Investigates mass killings where a single gender is singled out.

German Propaganda Archives
www.calvin.edu/cas/gpa
Who did you think you were kidding, Mr Hitler?

Global Ideas Bank
www.globalideasbank.org
If you think you know better than the politicians, come and post
your ideas for global change – who knows, they might even read it.

Grassroots.com
www.grassroots.com
Tracks (US) political action and election policies across the board,
aided by *TV Nation* champ Michael Moore, whose homepage is
also worth a look. Believe it or not, some people aren't so keen on
Moore's activities, see MooreWatch.com:
www.michaelmoore.com
www.moorewatch.com

Greenpeace International
www.greenpeace.org
Rebels with many a good cause.

Hindu Holocaust Museum
www.mantra.com/holocaust
Contends that the massacre of Hindus during Muslim rule in India
was of a scale unparalleled in history, yet it has largely gone undoc-
umented.

politics & government

InfoWar
www.infowar.com
Warfare issues from prank hacking to industrial espionage and military propaganda.

Jane's IntelWeb
http://intelweb.janes.com
Brief updates on political disturbances, terrorism, intelligence agencies and subterfuge worldwide. For a full directory of covert operations, see:
www.virtualfreesites.com/covert.html

Liberty
www.liberty-human-rights.org.uk
Championing human and civil rights in England and Wales. For a more global perspective, see Human Rights Watch:
www.hrw.org

National Charities Information Bureau
www.ncib.org
Investigate before you donate, both with NCIB and the Charity Commission. Once you're convinced, give at CharitiesDirect.com:
www.charity-commission.gov.uk
www.charitiesdirect.com

National Forum on People's Differences
www.yforum.com
Toss around touchy topics such as race, religion and sexuality with a sincerity that is normally tabooed by political politeness.

One World
www.oneworld.net
Collates news from over 350 global justice organizations.

Open Secrets
www.opensecrets.org
Track whose money is oiling the wheels of US politics. More keeping 'em honest at:
www.commoncause.org

Oxfam

www.oxfam.org
Pitch in to fight poverty and inequality. Also see:
www.roughguide-betterworld.com

Political Arena

www.planetquake.com/politicalarena/c2k.htm
Stage American elections on Quake.

The Political Graveyard

www.politicalgraveyard.com
Find out where over 81,000 politicians, diplomats and judges are
buried.

Political Leanings of Selected Cartoon Characters

www.unknown.nu/cartoon
Uncover the ideologies of those seemingly innocent Saturday morn-
ing fixtures.

Political Wire

http://politicalwire.com
In-depth political news aggregator that is US-heavy but which does
cover international politics as well.

Politics Online

www.PoliticsOnline.com
It may be subtitled "Fundraising and Internet tools for politics", but
this is actually a good general political site, with an emphasis on
how connectivity is changing the face of the game.

The Progressive Review

www.prorev.com
Washington's dirt dug up from all sides of the fence. For darker soil,
try the RealChange.org site:
www.realchange.org

Protest.net – A Calendar of Protest Worldwide

http://protest.net
Find a nearby riot you can call your own.

politics & government

Public Education Network
www.penpress.org
Frightening statistics about global inequality and political madness.

Spin On
www.spinon.co.uk
Play games such as "Stay to the Right of Jack Straw", "Egg Prescott" and the "Hague Goes Trucking Simulator".

Spunk Press
www.spunk.org
All the anarchy you'll ever need, organized neatly and with reassuring authority. More of the same can be found at:
www.infoshop.org

This Modern World
www.thismodernworld.com
Archive of Tom Tomorrow's scathing political cartoon.

Tolerance.org
www.tolerance.org
Shining the public flashlight on hate groups and political forces that threaten to undermine democracy and diversity. See also:
www.publiceye.org
www.splcenter.org

UK Census
www.statistics.gov.uk
More statistics on the UK and its citizens than you'd care to know.

US Presidential Candidates and their Evil Genes
www.nenavadno.com/usaelections2000.html
Biocybernetic criminals from the 33rd dimension take America.

YouGov
www.yougov.com
A good attempt at using the Internet to make government more accountable. There are columns and comment from John Humphrys, Fay Weldon and Ian Hargreaves, plus constantly updated political

news. The best features, though, are the People's Parliament, which allows users to vote on the same issues as parliament, a service to create e-petitions and GovDoctor, which identifies MPs, councillors and service managers.

ZNet
www.zmag.org
Fresh stuff from dissident writers around the world, including big names such as Chomsky.

Property

The Web is a great way to look for property to rent or buy. You can see hundreds of offerings in half an hour without even leaving your front room. Try the following sites as well as those of your local estate agents:

Accommodation Directory www.accommodation.com
Assertahome www.assertahome.com
Easier www.easier.co.uk
Find A Property www.findaproperty.com
Home Sale www.home-sale.co.uk
Homefile www.homefileuk.co.uk
Homepages www.homepages.co.uk
HouseWeb www.houseweb.co.uk
HouseNet www.housenet.co.uk
Let's Direct www.letsdirect.co.uk
LondonHomeNet www.londonhomenet.com
Pavilions of Splendour www.heritage.co.uk
Property Finder www.propertyfinder.co.uk
Property Live www.propertylive.co.uk
Property Watch www.propwatch.com
Property World www.propertyworld.com
Vebra www.vebra.com

property

For commercial property, try:

Comproperty www.comproperty.com

For help with getting the best mortgage see our **Money and Banking** section (p.162), or see what's recommended here:

Find www.find.co.uk
MoneySupermarket www.moneysupermarket.com/mortgages
UKMortgagesOnline www.ukmortgagesonline.com

British Association of Removers
www.removers.org.uk
Search for a mover who meets the BAR's standards of service.

Help I Am Moving
www.helpiammoving.com
Tries to remove the hassle from moving. Also try The Move Channel-and Really Moving:
www.themovechannel.com
www.reallymoving.com

Home Check
www.homecheck.co.uk
An excellent service for prospective home buyers: type in your future postcode and it will tell you if you need to worry about subsidence, pollution, air quality, flood risk or if the Triads are likely to firebomb the flat below.

ihavemoved.com
www.ihavemoved.com
Bulk-notify UK companies of your new address.

International Real Estate Digest
www.ired.com
This site helps you locate real estate listings, guides, and property-related services worldwide.

Islands for Sale
www.islandsforsale.com
Get away from it all. For more opportunities for isolation, try Tropical Islands or World of Private Islands:
www.tropical-islands.com
www.vladi-private-islands.de

National Security Inspectorate
www.nsi.org.uk
Keep tabs on the guys installing your alarm. To make sure your lock doesn't get picked, check out:
www.locksmiths.co.uk

Property Broker
www.propertybroker.co.uk
If you live within the M25 you can avoid the middleman and advertise your property here for a flat fee of £137.

UpMyStreet
www.upmystreet.com
Astounding wealth of house prices, health, crime, schools, tax and other statistics on UK neighbourhoods. Mighty useful if you're shifting base.

Radio & Webcasts

Not only do almost all radio stations have a website, most now pipe their transmissions online using RealAudio and/or Windows Media Format. Both players come with in-built station directories along with Web-based event guides that are fine for starting out, but nowhere near complete.

RealGuide http://realguide.real.com
Windows Media Guide http://windowsmedia.com

Not enough? Then buy the *Rough Guide to Internet Radio* or try one of the specialist radio directories, which list physical radio stations with websites along with full-time stations that exist only online, normally lumped together by country or genre. If they don't provide a direct link to the live feed, visit the station's site and look for a button or link that says "live" or "listen".

BRS Web Radio www.web-radio.fm
ComFM www.comfm.fr/live/radio
Live Radio www.live-radio.net
Radio Jump www.radiojump.com
Radio Locator www.radio-locator.com
RadioNow www.radio-now.co.uk
Shoutcast www.shoutcast.com
Virtual Tuner www.virtualtuner.com

Apart from the traditional single-stream broadcasters, dozens of sites host multiple feeds. These might be live, on demand, on rotation, archived or one-off events. They tend to work more like inflight entertainment than radio.

Air Bubble www.airbubble.com
Anime Hardcore http://animehardcore.net
Betalounge www.betalounge.com
CD Now www.cdnow.com/radio
House of Blues www.hob.com
Interface http://interface.pirate-radio.co.uk
Live 365 www.live365.com
Online Classics www.onlineclassics.net
Yahoo! Radio http://radio.yahoo.com

There are thousands upon thousands of webcasters sending their signals into the ether. These are some of the more familiar names and some of the oddest:

BBC Radio
www.bbc.co.uk/radio
Auntie online, with something for everyone.

BitBop Turner
www.audiomill.com
undergoing maintenance
Stupid name, but a great tool: download the software and it monitors online radio stations most likely to play your favourite songs, then records them for playback at your leisure.

De Concertzender
www.concertzender.nl
A real boon for lovers of "highbrow" music: jazz, classical and New Music from this Dutch terrestrial station.

MTV
www.mtv.com
It may not be radio, but it does have hundreds of video streams available.

Solid Steel
www.ninjatune.net/solidsteel
Coldcut have been airing their essential mixes since 1988 on various terrestrial stations; you can listen to almost all of them (with playlists) here.

Swank Radio
www.swankradio.com
Space-age bachelor pad muzak for cocktail enthusiasts and Tiki lovers everywhere.

Van Halen Radio Network
www.vhradio.com
Yup, all Van Halen, all the time.

radio & webcasts

WFMU
www.wfmu.org
Lucky residents of the New York metropolitan area have been able to call this treasure theirs for thirty-odd years. Now you can listen to the best freeform radio station on earth no matter where you live.

WNUR
www.wnur.org
Another great American station (from Chicago) covering experimental and local music better than nearly anyone else.

Xfm
www.xfm.co.uk
Catch London's indie station live online, all the time.

If you fancy setting up your own station or listening to the online equivalent of pirate radio, try:

Icecast.org www.icecast.org
Live365 www.live365.com

To promote your own station or search for a song or artist currently playing across thousands of others:

Crystal Radio
www.midnightscience.com
Build a simple wireless that needs no battery.

Interface Pirate Radio
www.pirate-radio.co.uk
address goes to interface.pirate-radio.org which is currently being updated
Attempting to bring the aural ambience of East London to the Net.

Phil's Old Radios
www.antiqueradio.org
If you've ever drifted to sleep bathed in the soft glow of a crackling Bakelite wireless, Phil's collection of vacuum-era portables may instantly flood you with childhood memories.

Pirate Radio
http://pirateradio.about.com
failed to load properly
Stake your claim on the airwaves. More piracy info at How to Be a Radio Pirate:
www.irational.org/sic/radio

Reference

There's really only one place to go these days if you want an answer fast, and that's **Wikipedia** – the encyclopedia you can be a part of. As with all "wikis", the entries of this amazing resource (quarter of a million and growing) are user-editable, so if you see a mistake or a misplaced semicolon, you can simply change it. This collaborative approach has created a surprisingly comprehensive and accurate multi-language encyclopedia, which, due to the "open-content" arrangement, will be freely available to the public until the end of time.

Wikipedia www.wikipedia.org

reference

With the Net threatening the very foundations of the encyclopedia industry, it should come as no surprise to find most of the
household names well entrenched online. While they're not all
entirely free, they're certainly cheaper and more up-to-date than
their bulky paper equivalents.

Britannica www.eb.com
Columbia www.bartleby.com/65
Encarta www.encarta.com
Macquarie www.macnet.mq.edu.au

Here's the best of the rest:

Acronym Finder
www.acronymfinder.com
Before you follow IBM, TNT and HMV into initializing your company's
name, make sure it doesn't mean something blue. More here:
www.ucc.ie/info/net/acronyms/acro.html

All Experts
www.allexperts.com
Ask any question and let unpaid experts do the thinking. For more
answers to those burning questions, try:
www.askme.com

Alternative Dictionary
www.notam.uio.no/~hcholm/altlang
Bucket your foreign chums in their mother tongue.

American ASL Dictionary
www.handspeak.com
Learn sign language through this site of simple animations.

Anagram Genius
www.anagramgenius.com
Recycle used letters.

Aphorisms Galore
www.ag.wastholm.net
Sound clever by repeating someone else's lines.

Babelfish Translator
http://babelfish.altavista.com/translate.dyn
Translate text, including webpages, in seconds. Though run some text
back and forth a few times and you'll end up with something that
wouldn't look out of place on a Japanese t-shirt.

Bartleby Reference
www.bartleby.com/reference
Free access to several contemporary and classic reference works
such as the American *Heritage* dictionaries, *Columbia Encyclopedia*,
Fowler's *King's English*, Emily Post's *Etiquette*, the *Cambridge History of
English and American Literature* and Gray's *Anatomy*.

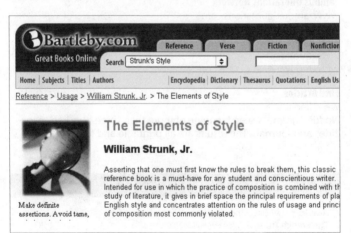

Biography
www.biography.com
Recounting more than 25,000 lives.

reference

Calculators Online
www.math.com
Awesome collection of online tools.

Cliché Finder
www.westegg.com/cliche
Submit a word or phrase to find out how not to use it.

Earthstation1
www.earthstation1.com
The twentieth century captured in sound and vision.

Encyclopedia Mythica
www.pantheon.org
Hefty album of mythology, folklore and legend.

Famous Quotations Network
www.famous-quotations.com
Perk up essays and letters with a witticism from Oscar Wilde or a Senegalese proverb. For more quotes, try:
www.quotationspage.com
www.motivational-quotes.com

Find Articles
www.findarticles.com
No fuss, no muss search engine of more than three hundred magazines and journals. The results are all printable and free.

Learn a language

Arabic http://i-cias.com/babel/arabic
The French Tutorial www.frenchlesson.com
German For Travellers www.germanfortravellers.com
The Japanese Tutor www.japanese-online.com
StudySpanish.com www.studyspanish.com
BBC www.bbc.co.uk/languages
Word Reference www.wordreference.com

GuruNet

www.gurunet.com

A powerful reference tool: type in a term and you'll immediately get definitions, pronunciation, explanations and more. Unfortunately, anything more than two weeks' use will cost you.

How Stuff Works

www.howstuffworks.com

Learn the secrets behind fake tans, animal camouflage and cable modems.

InfoPlease

www.infoplease.com

Handy, all-purpose almanac for stats and trivia.

Librarian's Index

www.lii.org

Naturally there are oodles of reference portals brimming with helpful reference tools. These are some of the best:

www.libraryspot.com

http://dmoz.org/Reference

www.refdesk.com

http://dir.yahoo.com/reference

Megaconverter 2

www.megaconverter.com/mega2

Calculate everything from your height in angstroms to the pellets of lead per ounce of buckshot needed to bring down an overcharging consultant.

Nonsensicon

www.nonsensicon.com

Non-existent words and their meanings.

Oxford Reference

www.oxfordreference.com

Mind-blowing reference library of some one hundred titles now online. Unfortunately, you have to subscribe.

reference

Questia
www.questia.com
A contender for the title of world's biggest library, this site has the full contents of nearly half a million books and journals.

Reality Clock
www.realityclock.com
An ever-expanding source of statistics, from the bizarre and shocking to the mundane.

RhymeZone
www.rhymezone.com
Get a hoof up in putting together a classy love poem.

Roget's Thesaurus
www.thesaurus.com
New format; useless as ever.

Skeptic's Dictionary
www.skepdic.com
Punch holes in mass-media funk and pseudosciences such as homeopathy, astrology and iridology.

The Straight Dope
www.straightdope.com
Cecil Adams's answers to hard questions. Find out how to renounce your US citizenship, what "Kemosabe" means and the difference between a warm smell of colitas and colitis.

Slang dictionaries

Playground Slang www.odps.cyberscriber.com
A Prisoner's Dictionary http://dictionary.prisonwall.org
Pseudo Dictionary www.pseudodictionary.com
Glossary of Hardboiled Slang www.miskatonic.org/slang.html

Strunk's Elements of Style
www.bartleby.com/141
The complete classic of English usage in a nutshell, though unfortunately not the latest edition. For more on grammar and style:
www.edunet.com/english/grammar
www.garbl.com

Symbols
www.symbols.com
Ever woken up with a strange sign tattooed on your buttocks? Here's where to find what it means without calling in Agent Mulder.

What is?
www.whatis.com
Unravel cumbersome computer and Internet jargon without having even more thrown at you. Also visit the wonderful Webopedia:
www.webopedia.com

Whoohoo
www.whoohoo.co.uk
If you come from Berwick and find yourself in the East End unable to understand a word anyone says, this site may be of help.

The Why Files
http://whyfiles.org
The science behind the headlines.

World Atlas
www.worldatlas.com
Maps, flags, latitude and longitude finder, population growth and so on – though you might prefer the maps on paper. For more see our Maps chapter (p.160), or try:
www.nationalgeographic.com/mapmachine
http://dmoz.org/Reference/Maps

World Factbook
www.odci.gov/cia/publications/factbook
Information for spies from the CIA.

Xrefer
www.xrefer.com
Consult this site to query a broad selection of prominent reference works from Oxford University Press, Houghton Mifflin, Penguin, Macmillan, Bloomsbury and Market House Books.

Yellow Pages
www.yell.com
If you're too lazy to flip through the book.

YourDictionary.com
www.yourdictionary.com
For one-point access to over a thousand dictionaries across almost every language. Try also Dictionary.com and One Look:
www.dictionary.com
www.onelook.com

Relationships, Dating & Friendship

The Internet is the biggest singles bar humankind has ever created: with millions and millions of users from around the world, even the most lovelorn are bound to find someone worth cyber-flirting with. However, it's worth bearing in mind that the World Wide Web is no different from the real world and there are plenty of scam artists, hustlers, leeches and other unsavoury characters lurking in unsuspected corners. By all means enjoy dropping virtual handkerchiefs to perspective suitors, but keep your wits about you. Before engaging in any social intercourse on the Net, go to Wildx Angel (www.wildxangel.com) for advice on the safest way to go on the pull online.

To help you on your way, here are some of the Web's biggest dating agencies:

Dateline www.dateline.co.uk
Dating Direct www.datingdirect.com
Elite Dating www.elite-dating.co.uk
Friendfinder www.friendfinder.com
Lavalife www.lavalife.com
Lovefinder www.lovefinder.co.uk
Match.com www.match.com
SocialNet www.relationships.com
UDate www.udate.com
UK Singles www.uksingles.co.uk

To find a chat room, try a chat portal such as:

The Chat Room Directory www.webarrow.net/chatindex
Chatseek http://chatseek.com
Chat Shack Network http://chatshack.net
The Ultimate Chatlist www.chatlist.com

For more, try the Open Directory's chat portal list:

Open Directory http://dmoz.org/Computers/Internet/Chat

Cyberspace Inmates
www.cyberspace-inmates.com
Strike up an email romance with a prison inmate – maybe even one
on Death Row.

Everything you say or do

Cyberspace Inmates

Rehabilitation Through Correspondence

relationships, dating & friendshipt

Dating Directories
www.singlesites.com
Come aboard, they're expecting you.

The Divorce Support Page
www.divorcesupport.com
Lots of friendly ears and shoulders to cry on.

Friends Reunited
www.friendsreunited.co.uk
You haven't forgotten. Now track them down one by one. More people who teased you in the common room are at:
www.classmates.com

Gentle, Romantic Woman Seeks Agnostic or Atheist for Strong Attraction, Friendship, Eventual Marriage and Deepest Love
http://hometown.aol.com/mary1777/index.htm
Middle-aged divorcée lays down the law.

The Hugging Site
http://members.tripod.com/~hugging
The history of embracing, hugging stories and tips to improve your cuddling technique.

Javina's Prostitution FAQ
www.javina.com/JJ3/faq.html
Learn the truth behind the *Pretty Woman* fantasy.

Love Calculator
www.lovecalculator.com
Enter your respective names to see if you're compatible.

Pen Pal Directory
http://dir.yahoo.com/Social_Science/Communications/Writing/Correspondence/Pen_Pals
Exchange email with strangers.

The Hugging Site (Halia suomeksi)

Most of us have some type of difficulties in expressing ourselves or we just don't share our feelings enough with the people next to us. Often it's all because our western culture has this peculiar way to emphasize solidness and individualism in our behaviour. One way to enrich communication, and at the side the best and sometimes even the worst parts of our lives, is hugging.

The Rejection Line
www.lazystudent.co.uk/rejectline.html
Let the professionals break it to that not-so-special someone.

Romance 101
www.rom101.com
Chat-up lines, compatibility tests and advice from men to women such as "Never buy a 'new' brand of beer because 'it was on sale.'"

Secret Admirer
www.secretadmirer.com
Find out whether your secret crush digs you back. More stalking at:
www.ecrush.com

So There
www.sothere.com
A place to post your parting shots.

relationships, dating & friendship

Swoon
www.swoon.com
Dating, mating and relating.
Courtesy of Condé Nast's
Details, *GQ*, *Glamour*, and
Mademoiselle.

Tips for Dating Emotional Cripples
www.grrl.com/bipolar.html
The site all women must visit.

Vampire Exchange
www.vein-europe.demon.co.uk
Give blood as an act of love. Lose another armful here:
www.sanguinarius.org

Way Too Personal
www.waytoopersonal.com
Wild and woolly adventures in Internet dating.

Social networks

Touted by many as the next big Internet revolution, social networks are designed to cultivate every type of relationship, from friendship and romance to business partnerships. They're based on the idea of "degrees of separation". You set up a list of your friends or colleagues and invite them to join and do the same. Soon a network is established where you can make contact with people you may not know directly, but you know are "friends of friends", "friends of friends of friends", and so on. Most also include sub-networks combining people of similar interests, occupations and the like.

Many such networks are still pretty IT- and new-media focused, but more are appearing all the time. Here are a few of the bigger networking sites worth visiting:

Orkut www.orkut.com
Tribe www.tribe.net
Ecademy www.ecademy.com

Weddings in the Real World
www.theknot.com
Prepare to jump the broom – or untie the knot:
www.divorcesource.com
www.absolutedivorce.com
www.hell2u.com/divorce.htm

Religion

If you haven't yet signed up with a religious sect or are unhappy with the one passed down by your folks, here's your opportunity to survey the field at your own pace. Most are open to newcomers, though certain rules and conditions may apply. For a reasonably complete and unbiased breakdown of faith dealerships, try:

BeliefNet www.beliefnet.com
Comparative Religion www.academicinfo.net/religindex.html
Religious Tolerance www.religioustolerance.org

But don't expect such an easy ride from those demanding proof:

Atheism http://atheism.miningco.com
Christian Burner www.christianburner.com
The Secular Web www.infidels.org

If you really can't make up your mind, or you just fancy a giggle, try a few of these sites:

Adherents.com
www.adherents.com
Statistical ranking of the world's religions from the Aaronic Order to Zurvanism.

Anglicans Online
http://anglicansonline.org
A gentle catapult into the Church of England worldwide.

religion

Avatar Search
www.AvatarSearch.com
Search the occult Net for spiritual guidance and lottery tips.

The Bible Gateway
http://bible.gospelcom.net
Set your table with the Good Book.

The Brick Testament
www.thereverend.com/brick_testament
And on the eighth day God created Lego…

A Brief History of the Apocalypse
www.abhota.info
It takes a lickin' and keeps on tickin'.

The British Druid Order
www.druidorder.demon.co.uk
Dance around Stonehenge, make potions and meet fellow wizards.

BuddhaNet
www.buddhanet.net
Take a ride on the wheel of dharma and download the Diamond
Sutra.

Catholic Church – God's One and Only Church
www.truecatholic.org
More troops armed with the truth.

Catholic Online
www.catholic.org
Saints, angels, shopping, discussion and a portal to the online territory occupied by Catholics.

Celebrity Atheist List
www.celebatheists.com
Big names you won't spot in Heaven.

Cheesy Jesus
www.cheesyjesus.com
Buy gadgets to bring you closer to God.

Chick
www.chick.com
Hardcore Christian pornography.

Christian Answers
http://christiananswers.net
Movies and computer games reviewed and hard questions answered, by Christians who know what's good for you.

Christians vs. Muslims
http://debate.org.uk
Put your faith on the line. More debate to be found here:
www.rim.org/muslim/islam.htm
http://members.aol.com/AllahIslam
www.answering-islam.org
www.muslim-answers.org

Church of England
www.cofe.anglican.org
The home of Anglicanism online. Presbyterians should head north of the border at Church of Scotland.
www.churchofscotland.org.uk

religion

Church of the Subgenius
www.subgenius.com
Find the truth through slackness.

CrossSearch
www.crosssearch.com
Find Christian groups of all denominations.

Crosswalk
www.crosswalk.com
Catch up with the latest on Jesus.

Demon Possession Handbook
http://diskbooks.org/hs.html
Train for a job with the Watcher's Council.

Exorcism
www.logoschristian.org/exorcism.html
Don't try this at home.

Free Deliverance
www.demonbuster.com
Use Jesus's teachings to cast out demons, wage spiritual warfare and overcome bipolar disorder, depression, addiction, obesity and other modern ailments.

The Hindu Universe
www.hindunet.org
Hindu dharma – the philosophy, culture and customs.

The Holy See
www.vatican.va
Official hideout of the new pope (the one that looks like Emperor
Palpatine) and his posse, see:
www.flickr.com/photos/yaaaay/10092479

Islamic Gateway
www.ummah.net
Get down with Muhammed (*sallallahu `alaihi wa sallam*). Also:
www.musalman.com
www.fatwa-online.com

Jesus of the Week
www.jesusoftheweek.com
The original Mr Nice Guy in 52 coy poses per year. Catch him wink-
ing at you here:
www.winkingjesus.com

Latter Day Designs Vinyl Figures
www.lehi.com/vin1.html
Action figures from The Book of Mormon.

The Mark of the Beast
www.greaterthings.com/essays/666mark.htm
Did you know that "Holy Bible" is "666" in ASCII code?

Miracles Page
www.mcn.org/1/miracles
Spooky signs that point towards a cosmic conspiracy.

OrishaNet
www.orishanet.org
Learn about the Cuban religion of Santeria and consult with Oshun,
Ifá and Elegba.

The Pagan Library
www.paganlibrary.com
Pagan and Wiccan texts and other information on the mysteries of this
ancient craft.

religion

Peyote Way Church of God
www.peyoteway.org
Unless you're Native American or live in select southern US states, you stand to be locked up for finding God through the psychedelic cactus. Otherwise, feel free to fry your brain; just don't drive home from church.

The Peyote Way Church

A non-denominational All Race Peyotist Organization

Since 1978

Enter Here

Roy Taylor Ministries
www.roytaylorministries.com
"American Pie" is God's song and other examples of questionable hermeneutics.

Satanism 101
www.satanism101.com
Enter this address and go straight to Hell:
www.what-the-hell-is-hell.com
www.virtualhell.net

Scientology
www.scientology.org.uk
The favoured religion of Hollywood stars.

Shamanism
http://deoxy.org/shaman.htm
Entheogens, plant sacraments and other ecstatic vehicles.

Ship of Fools: the Magazine of Christian Unrest
http://ship-of-fools.com
The lighter side of Christianity.

Skeptics Annotated Bible
www.skepticsannotatedbible.com
Contends that the Good Book is a misnomer.

Stories of the Dreaming
www.dreamtime.net.au
Selection of enchanting bedtime stories in text, video and audio
that explain creation from an Aboriginal perspective. Don't believe
in creation? Go tell it to the jury:
www.talkorigins.org

Totally Jewish
www.totallyjewish.com
Spiritual guidance and community portal for the chosen people.
More good mozel at:
www.chosen-people.com
www.maven.co.il
www.jewishnet.co.uk

Universal Life Church
http://ulc.org
Become a self-ordained minister.

science

The Vodou Page
http://members.aol.com/racine125
Learn how to convene with the loas.

The Witches' Voice
www.witchvox.com
Expresses a burning desire to correct misinformation about witch-craft, a legally recognized religion in the US since 1985.

Zen
www.do-not-zzz.com
Take a five-minute course in meditation.

Science

To keep abreast of science news and developments stop by **Scitech**, which aggregates stories from the leading scientific media:

Scitech Daily Review www.scitechdaily.com

Or go straight to one of the numerous science journals, many of which let you sign up for daily, weekly or monthly news emails:

Archeology www.archaeology.org
British Medical Journal www.bmj.com
Bulletin of Atomic Scientists www.bullatomsci.org
Discover www.discover.com
Discovery Channel www.discovery.com
Edge www.edge.org
Highwire Press http://highwire.stanford.edu
The Lancet www.thelancet.com
National Geographic www.nationalgeographic.com
New Scientist www.newscientist.com
Popular Mechanics www.popularmechanics.com
Popular Science www.popsci.com

Science à GoGo www.scienceagogo.com
Science Magazine www.sciencemag.org
Science News www.sciencenews.org
Scientific American www.scientificamerican.com
The Scientist www.the-scientist.com
Skeptical Inquirer www.csicop.org/si
Technology Review www.techreview.com

Looking for a something specific or a range of sites within a strand? Try browsing or searching a directory:

Hypography www.hypography.com
Open Directory http://dmoz.org/Science
SciSeek www.sciseek.com
Treasure Troves of Science www.treasure-troves.com
Yahoo http://dir.yahoo.com/science

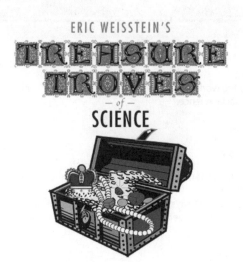

science

Albert Einstein Online
www.westegg.com/einstein
In essence an Albert Einstein portal, with links to biographies, quotes, articles and essays, photos and other pages related to *Time* magazine's Man of the Century.

Amusement Park Physics
www.learner.org/exhibits/parkphysics
If your kid has absolutely no interest in potential and kinetic energy, send them to this fantastic site for the coolest science lesson on the Web, and give them the chance to design their own rollercoaster.

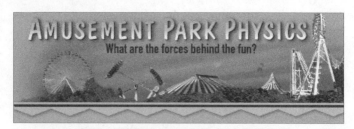

AnthroNet
www.anthro.net
Gateway to the world of anthropology, archeology and other subjects in the field of social science.

Battlebots
www.battlebots.com
Robots kick ass.

The Braintainment Center
www.brain.com
Start with a test that says you're not so bright, then prove it by buying loads of self-improvement gear. Try some more here:
www.iqtest.com
www.mind-gear.com
www.mindmedia.com

Chemistry.org.uk
www.liv.ac.uk/Chemistry/Links/link.html
The chemistry section of the WWW Virtual Library has some 8500 links to chemistry sites. Advanced chemists should check out ChemWeb (www.chemweb.com) and its Available Chemical Directory of 278,000 compounds (you need to subscribe to gain access).

Cool Robot of the Week
http://ranier.hq.nasa.gov/telerobotics_page/coolrobots.html
Clever ways to get machines to do our dirty work. For a directory of simulators, combat comps, clubs and DIY bots, direct your agent to: www.robotcafe.com

Dangerous Laboratories
www.dangerouslaboratories.org
Definitely don't try this at home.

Flat Earth Society
www.flat-earth.org
Proving five hundred years of science wrong.

Genewatch
www.genewatch.org
Dusting crops for genetic fingerprints.

Gray's Anatomy Online
www.bartleby.com/107
The complete edition of the essential anatomical text.

science

History of Mathematics
www-groups.dcs.st-andrews.ac.uk/~history
The life and times of various bright sparks with numbers.

HotAir – Annals of Improbable Research
www.improbable.com
Science gone too far, or around the bend. Includes the Ig Nobel awards for achievements that cannot, or should not, be reproduced.

How Does a Thing Like That Work?
www.pitt.edu/~dwilley/Show/menu.html
Entertaining physics demonstration experiments.

How Stuff Works
www.howstuffworks.com
Unravel the mysterious machinations behind all sorts of stuff from Christmas to cruise missiles.

Interactive Frog Dissection
http://teach.virginia.edu/go/frog
Pin down a frog, grab your scalpel and follow the pictures.

The Lab
www.abc.net.au/science
ABC science news and program info with Q&As from Aussie pop-science superstar, Dr Karl Kruszelnicki.

MadSciNet: 24-hour Exploding Laboratory
www.madsci.org
Collective of more than a hundred scientific smarty-pantses set up specifically to answer your dumb questions. More at:
www.ducksbreath.com
www.wsu.edu/DrUniverse
www.sciam.com/askexpert
www.sciencenet.org.uk

MIT Media Labs
www.media.mit.edu
If you've read *Being Digital* or any of Nicholas Negroponte's *Wired* columns, you'll know he has some pretty tall ideas about our electronic future. Here's where he gets them.

National Inventors Hall of Fame
www.invent.org
Homepage of a museum based in Akron, Ohio, dedicated to the world's most important inventors. Includes short biographies and pictures of luminaries such as Thomas Edison, Enrico Fermi and Louis Pasteur. For more modern inventions, go to Inventions And Technologies:
www.inventions-tech.com/epanel.htm
And for questionable inventions see Patently Absurd!:
www.patent.freeserve.co.uk

Netsurfer Science
www.netsurf.com/nss
Subscribe to receive weekly bulletins on science and technology sites.

Nobel e-Museum
http://nobelprize.org
Read all about Nobel prize-winners.

science

Rocketry Online
www.rocketryonline.com
Take on NASA at its own game.

Skeptics Society
www.skeptic.com
Don't try to pull a swift one on this crowd.

The Soundry
http://library.thinkquest.org/19537
A fun introduction to the science of acoustics.

Strange Science: The Rocky Road to Modern Paleontology and Biology
www.strangescience.net
A great site exploring the fallout of science's paradigm wars.

Time Travel
http://freespace.virgin.net/steve.preston
"We discuss many of the common objections to time travel and we show that these objections are without foundation."

Volcano World
http://volcano.und.nodak.edu
Monitor the latest eruptions, see photos of every major volcano in the world, and virtually tour a Hawaiian smoky.

VoltNet
www.voltnet.com
Celebrate the power of electricity by blowing things up.

WebElements
www.webelements.com
Click on an element in the periodic table and suss it out in depth.
www.chemsoc.org/viselements

Weird Science and Mad Scientists
www.eskimo.com/~billb/weird.html
Free energy, Tesla, anti-gravity, aura, cold fusion, parapsychology
and other strange scientific projects and theories.

Why Files
http://whyfiles.news.wisc.edu
Entertaining reports on the science behind current news.

Shopping

If you can't buy it on the Web, it probably doesn't exist, but shopping sites range from the great to the gruesome, so it pays to look
around before tapping in your credit-card details. For obscure
things, you'll probably need to locate a specialist online store. To
do this, you could either try a carefully phrased **Google** search
– adding "price" or "buy" helps bring up the retail sites – or
consult one of the online shopping directories:

Buyers' Guide www.buyersguide.to
UK Shopping www.ukshopping.com
UK Shop Search www.ukshopsearch.com

For more common items, you may want to try a shopping bot:
enter a product name or keyword and it'll return a listing of
prices and availability across a range of retailers. Of course, a
bargain-finder is only as good as its sources, so it often pays to

try more than one. Major UK bots include:

Checkaprice www.checkaprice.com
Dealtime www.dealtime.com
Easy Value www.easyvalue.com
Kelkoo http://uk.kelkoo.com
Price Checker www.PriceChecker.co.uk
The Price Guide UK www.price-guide.co.uk

For price and service comparisons of mobile phone, credit card, electricity, water and gas suppliers, try:

Buy.co.uk www.buy.co.uk
UK Energy www.ukenergy.co.uk
U Switch www.uswitch.com

Of course, before you buy anything big, you'll probably want to do some research into the product itself, and the Net is one of the best places to look. Either try **Usenet** or one of the many websites that offer buying guides, customer opinions, ratings and links to external reviews. Perhaps the most thorough collection is:

Productopia www.productopia.com

But there's plenty more advice at:

Consumer Review www.consumerreview.com
Dooyoo www.dooyoo.com
Epinions www.epinions.com
eSmarts www.esmarts.com
Google Groups http://groups.google.com
Rateitall.com www.rateitall.com

And there's always **Which?** for trustworthy consumer advice:

Which? www.which.net

BizRate
www.bizrate.com
Shopping sites rated and reviewed.

Catalogue City
http://uk.catalogcity.com
If you're unconvinced by online shopping and would prefer it on paper, drive your postie crazy by ordering every catalogue in the world. For even more junk mail, try Buyers' Index, Catalink and Catalog Site:
www.buyersindex.com
www.catalink.co.uk
http://catalogsite.catalogcity.com

shopping

Buying flowers

First, visit **About Flowers** (www.aboutflowers.com) to find out the meanings of flowers and the right ones for various occasions. Then place your order at:

Clare Florist www.clareflorist.co.uk
A Which? webtrader offering a good range of bouquets.

Daisys2Roses www.daisys2roses.com
Despite a slight design flaw, this site allows you to create your own bouquet, a service which almost no other online florist offers.

0800flowers.com www.0800flowers.com
Offers an impressively wide range of bouquets.

Interflora www.interflora.co.uk
Interflora may be the biggest name in flowers, but their site is pretty run-of-the-mill. Aside from reliability and name recognition, its main feature is a personal organizer that will remind you of anniversaries and birthdays.

Teleflorist www.teleflorist.co.uk
Like most of the big players, Teleflorist's site seems to offer a fairly limited range of bouquets and arrangements.

Consumer World
www.consumerworld.org
Not all of the information here may be appropriate because it's an American site, but this should be an automatic bookmark for anyone intending to do any shopping either on- or offline. Aside from the comparison engines, bargain listings and product reviews, it has alerts on the latest scams and annoying marketing practices.

FreeCycle
http://freecycle.org
Why spend money when you can "freecycle"? The basic idea is that you get on your local group's mailing list, advertise anything useful that was heading for the bin and then pass it on for free if anyone's interested and take stuff off other people if you're interested. Search Google for your nearest scheme; London's can be found here:
http://groups.yahoo.com/group/FreecycleLondon

How to Complain
www.howtocomplain.com
Let the professionals do it for you.

LetsBuyIt.com
www.letsbuyit.com
This site uses collaborative buying power to clinch lower prices for its members across Europe.

MyGeek
www.mygeek.com
Type in your shopping request here and they will approach several different merchants looking for the best price.

PriceWatch
www.pricewatch.com
If you're after computer products, this shopping bot is one of the best comparison engines on the Web. Also try:
http://shopper.cnet.com

Silver Surfers

BBC Health: Health at 50
www.bbc.co.uk/health/50plus
Easily among the best of the BBC sites, largely because – unlike most of the Beeb's pages – it's not dependent on Auntie's programming. The advice is honest and there are no bells or whistles.

FiftyOn
www.fiftyon.co.uk
A portal for 50-pluses, with its best and most laudable feature being the advice and vacancies database it maintains for older jobseekers.

Hell's Geriatrics
www.hellsgeriatrics.co.uk
Grow old disgracefully.

silver surfers

I Don't Feel 50
www.idf50.co.uk
A fun, irreverent site run by Graham Andrews, with topics such as "Is Age Concern too Old?" and "Mind the Generation Gap".

National U3A UK
www.u3a.org.uk
Continuing adult education from the Third Age Trust and the University of the Third Age.

Retirement Matters
www.retirement-matters.co.uk
Online magazine specializing in news, reviews and information for over-50s.

Saga Magazine
www.saga.co.uk/magazine
Homepage of the magazine for over 50s, with content from the current issue, although there is no archive of past articles.

Senior Site
www.seniorsite.com
American online community for grown-ups, with Pat Boone as the entertainment correspondent and an excellent section on protecting yourself against "senior scams".

Seniority.co.uk
www.seniority.co.uk
Like all online communities, this one for senior citizens is only as good as its contributors. While some of Seniority is hit-and-miss, it does have an impressive community spirit.

SeniorsSearch
www.seniorssearch.com
Search engine dedicated to resources for silver surfers.

Third Age
www.thirdage.com
This American online magazine for older women may look like some terrible advert for feminine hygiene products, but underneath the terrible design is an informative, friendly e-zine.

Write a Senior Citizen
www.writeseniors.com
Penpals for seniors.

Space

If you have more than a passing interest in space go straight to the source:

British National Space Centre www.bnsc.gov.uk
European Space Agency www.esrin.esa.it
NASA www.nasa.gov
Royal Greenwich Observatory www.rog.nmm.ac.uk

Or try any of these specialist space ports:

Amateur Astronomy Magazine www.amateurastronomy.com
Astronomy.com www.astronomy.com
Astronomy Now www.astronomynow.com
Human Spaceflight http://spaceflight.nasa.gov
Jet Propulsion Lab www.jpl.nasa.gov

space

Planetary Society http://planetary.org
Sky & Telescope Magazine www.skypub.com
Space.com www.space.com
Space Daily www.spacedaily.com
SpaceRef www.spaceref.com
Universe Today www.universetoday.com

Alien Scalpel
www.alienscalpel.com
Protect yourself against abduction.

AstroCappella
www.astrocappella.com
Learn astronomy through great tunes such as "Doppler Shifting" and "Habitable Zone".

Astronomy Picture of the Day
http://antwrp.gsfc.nasa.gov/apod/astropix.html
Enjoy a daily helping of space served up by a gourmet astrochef.

Auroral Activity
www.sec.noaa.gov/pmap
Instantly see the current extent and position of the auroral oval above each pole.

Auroras: Paintings in the Sky
www.exploratorium.edu/learning_studio/auroras
If you're ever lucky enough to see the Aurora during a solar storm, you'll never take the night sky for granted again. The Exploratorium does a commendable job in explaining a polar phenomenon that very few people understand. More at:
www.alaskascience.com/aurora.htm

Bad Astronomy
www.badastronomy.com
Ditch your lifetime's supply of space misconceptions and clichés.

Chandra X-Ray
www.chandra.harvard.edu
Telescope's-eye view of black holes and supernovas.

Comets & Meteor Showers
http://comets.amsmeteors.org
Be on the lookout for falling rocks.

Darksky
www.darksky.org
Join the campaign against wanton street lighting. You'll see why in the gallery.

Deep Cold
www.deepcold.com
Artistic mockups of chic space racers that never left the hangar.

space

Earth Viewer
www.fourmilab.ch/earthview
View the earth in space and time.

Eclipse Cam
http://eclipse.span.ch/liveshow.htm
You don't even need a special box designed by your science teacher to view this site.

Galactic Information Service
http://home.c2i.net/galactic/torealf
"Here you will find information about the technology of the space-people."

Heavens Above
www.heavens-above.com
Correctly identify nearby satellites and space stations.

Hubblesite
http://hubble.stsci.edu
Intergalactic snapshots fresh from the Hubble telescope.

Hypothetical Planets
http://seds.lpl.arizona.edu/nineplanets/nineplanets/hypo.html
Paul Schylter's history of planets that have vanished or perhaps existed only in the minds of pre-Hubble scientists.

Inconstant Moon
www.inconstantmoon.com
Click on a date and see what's showing on the moon.

Intelligent Life on Mars
http://go.to/intelligentlifeonmars
The little green men know quantum physics.

International Star Registry
www.name-a-star.org.uk
Raise your flag in outer space.

Mars Home Page
http://mpfwww.jpl.nasa.gov
Get a bit more red dirt live from NASA's space safari and check out
the neighbours at MarsNews before you stake out your first plot at
MarsShop:
www.marsnews.com
www.marsshop.com

Mars Society UK
www.marssociety.org.uk
British chapter of an organization dedicated to getting humans to visit
the planet Mars.

MrEclipse
www.mreclipse.com
Dabble in the occultations.

space

The Nine Planets
www.ex.ac.uk/Mirrors/nineplanets
Bill Arnett's impressive multimedia tour of our solar system.

Planet Search
http://exoplanets.org
Info on planets in and outside our solar system.

Retro Aerospace
www.retro.com
Recycling simpler, sturdier rockets to make space travel more accessible to the common man.

Rocket Guy
www.rocketguy.com
The homepage of Brian Walker who plans to shoot himself thirty miles into the atmosphere. Wish him luck.

Seti@home
http://setiathome.ssl.berkeley.edu
Donate your processing resources to the non-lunatic end of the search for extraterrestrial intelligence by downloading a screen-saver that analyses data from the Arecibo radio telescope. Progress reports at:
www.seti.org
http://planetary.org
http://seti.uws.edu.au

Solar System Simulator
http://space.jpl.nasa.gov
Shift camp around the solar system until you find the best view.

Space Adventures
www.spaceadventures.com
If you've got $20 million lying around, you could become the next Dennis Tito. For the more modest of means, this site offers zero-gravity flights and personalized spacesuits just in case.

Space Calendar
www.jpl.nasa.gov/calendar
Guide to upcoming anniversaries, rocket launches, meteor showers, eclipses, asteroid and planet viewings and other happenings in the intergalactic calendar.

Space Weather
www.spaceweather.com
Monitor the influence of solar activity on the earth's magnetic field.

Star Stuff
www.starstuff.com
Beginner's guides to astronomy for kids.

Sport

For live calls, scores, tables, draws, teams, injuries and corruption enquiries across major sports, try the newspaper sites (p.197), breaking news services (p198) or sporting specialists such as:

Eurosport www.eurosport.com
SkySports www.skysports.com
Sportal (INT) www.sportal.com
Sporting Life www.sporting-life.com
Sports.com (Euro) http://sports.com

But if your interest even slightly borders on obsession you'll find far more satisfaction on the pages of something more one-eyed. For clubs and fan sites, drill down through **Yahoo!** and the **Open Directory**. They won't carry everything, but what you'll find will lead you to the right forces:

Open Directory http://dmoz.org/Sports
Yahoo! Sports http://dir.yahoo.com/recreation/sports

sport

If you can't get to the telly or are looking for webcasts of that crucial Rymans League derby, check **Sport On Air** for listings of streaming audio coverage on the Web.:

Sport On Air www.sportonair.com

If you are after in-depth news, reviews, listings and results for more specific sports, try one of these pages:

American Football
www.nfl.com
www.nfluth.com

Athletics
www.athletix.org

Baseball
www.mlb.com
www.baseball1.com

Basketball
www.nba.com

Boxing
www.secondsout.com

Cricket
www.cricinfo.com
www.334notout.com
www.wisden.com

Cycling
www.cyclingnews.com
www.cyclesource.co.uk
www.mtbbritain.co.uk

Football
www.footballgroundguide.co.uk
www.football365.com
www.4thegame.com
www.onefootball.com
www.rivals.net
www.soccerassociation.com
htpp://soccernet.espn.go.com
www.wsc.co.uk
www.soccerbase.com
www.teamtalk.com

Golf
www.golfweb.com
www.lpga.com
www.onlinegolf.co.uk

Motorsport
www.atlasf1.com
www.formula1.com
www.fia.com
www.indyracingleague.com
www.motograndprix.com
www.nascar.com
www.worldmotorsport.com
www.worldrally.net

Rugby
www.planet-rugby.com
www.rleague.com
www.ozleague.com
www.scrum.com

Sailing
www.smartguide.com
www.madforsailing.com

Skiing
www.skicentral.com
www.skiclub.co.uk
www.twsnow.com
www.snowboarding.com

Snooker
www.110sport.com/snooker

Surfing
www.surflink.com
www.britsurf.co.uk
www.eyeball-surfcheck.co.uk
www.6ftoffshore.com
www.coastalwatch.com

Swimming
www.swimmersworld.com
www.webswim.com

Tennis
www.tennis.com
www.wimbledon.org

Telecoms

Directory Enquiries
www.2bt.com/edq_resnamesearch
BT's directory enquiries site. For other British phone searches, try:
www.192.com
www.infospace.com
www.newdirectoryenquiries.com
www.118080.co.uk
www.yell.com

Efax
www.efax.com
Free up a phone line by receiving your faxes by email. Also worth investigating are:
www.j2.com
www.tpc.int

Internet telephony

Most instant messaging programs allow you to make video and audio calls to other users of the same programs, in effect offering free international phone calls between any two people with computer, broadband, microphone and speakers.

But it's also possible to make calls to regular and mobile telephones via your broadband connection. This isn't free, but it's usually much better value than using the old-fashioned telephone. No-commitment services such as Skype, for example, let you buy a €10 voucher and use it to call phones around the world. You could call a land line in Italy or a mobile in the US for around 1p per minute.

Skype www.skype.com

Other so-called VoIP (Voice Over IP) services are subscription based, offering a set number of national or international calls per month. For example:

Vonage www.vonage.co.uk
BT Broadband Voice www.btbroadbandvoice.com

MobileWorld
www.mobileworld.org
Assorted info on mobile phones and cellular networks.

The Payphone Project
www.payphone-project.com
An utterly bizarre site devoted to that near-extinct dinosaur of twentieth-century technology, the payphone. Includes payphone news, history of the payphone, photos and numbers. For more payphone numbers, try the Pay Phone Directory:
www.payphone-directory.org

Reverse Phone Directory
www.reversephonedirectory.com
Key in a US phone number to find its owner. For UK locations see:
www.ukphoneinfo.com

Splash Mobile
www.SplashMobile.com
Ring tones, logos, games and other essential accessories for your mobile. The site pays fees to the MCPS, so you can rest assured that the composer of the *Knight Rider* theme will get his just royalties. Other ringtone sites:
www.jippii.co.uk
www.mobiletones.com
www.phoneringsong.com
www.ringtones.co.uk
www.mob.tv
www.yourmobile.com

telecoms

WAP sites

If you've got a WAP phone or just like to pretend that you do (get a WAP emulator which enables your PC to read WML-encoded script at http://updev.phone.com), these are some of the best sites:

Ananova www.ananova.com
Get breaking news sent as customized WAP pages to your phone.

Ents24 www.ents24.co.uk
What's-on listings for the entire country.

Genie www.genie.co.uk
Get up-to-the-minute sports results.

Mail2Wap www.mail2wap.com
Collect your POP3 mail on a WAP phone.

Mobile WAP www.mobilewap.com
The largest WAP search engine.

Pocket Doctor www.pocketdoctor.co.uk/wap
Never forget to take your medicine, or get symptom descriptions sent to your mobile.

Railtrack http://railtrack.kizoom.co.uk
Why talk to an operator at the National Rail Enquiries line when you can have the info zapped to your phone instead? To check out how long your delay on the Tube will be, go to:
www.tflwap.gov.uk

Retrotopia Wireless Intellivision
www.intellivisionlives.com/retrotopia/wireless.shtml
Play 1980s classics like Astrosmash and Night Stalker on your mobile phone.

WAP Translator http://langues.ifrance.com/langues/index.wml
Translate to and from English, French, Italian, Spanish, German and Dutch with your phone.

UK STD Codes
www.brainstorm.co.uk/uk_std_code_search.htm
Keep up to date with the labrynthine complexities of the UK's phone exchanges.

UK.Telecom FAQ
www.gbnet.net/net/uk-telecom
Satisfy your curiosity about the British phone network.

What Does Your Phone Number Spell?
www.phonespell.org
Enter your phone number to see what it spells. The reverse lookup might help you choose a number.

World Time & Dialling Codes
www.whitepages.com.au/wp/search/time.html
International dialling info from anywhere to anywhere, including current times and area codes.

Television

Most TV stations maintain excellent sites with all kinds of extras such as live sports coverage and documentary follow-ups. We won't need to give you their addresses because they'll be flashing them at you at every opportunity.

For personalized listings, perhaps delivered by email, try your local **Yahoo!** or:

Ananova www.ananova.com/tv
OnTheBox.com www.onthebox.com

The best of these, however, is **Digiguide** (www.digiguide.co.uk) which is a customizable listings database that covers terrestrial, cable, digital and satellite. You download the site's free software, tell the program which region you live in and then download the next two weeks' worth of listings.

television

Bigglethwaite.com
www.bigglethwaite.com
With its comprehensive links page to UK TV websites, this is a good place to start any search.

DigiReels
www.digireels.co.uk
If you can't get enough of them on TV, then point your browser here immediately and search a mind-blowing database of over 100,000 adverts. Also check out UK Television Adverts:
www.uktvadverts.com

Drew's Script-O-Rama
www.script-o-rama.com/snazzy/tvscript.html
A huge set of links to an astonishing array of predominantly American television scripts and episode transcripts. Also try:
www.simplyscripts.com

Epguides
http://epguides.com
If you're serious about TV – really, really serious – this site is your holy grail. Containing complete episode guides for over 1700 shows (mostly American), which are linked to the Internet Movie Database for cross-referencing, this is an amazing research tool for academics, journalists, enthusiasts and general freaks. For similar coverage of Britcoms, try one of these sites:
www.phill.co.uk
www.episodeguides.com
www.televisionwithoutpity.com

Independent TeleWeb
www.itw.org.uk
The history of independent commercial television in the UK.

Jump The Shark
www.jumptheshark.com
Named after that episode in *Happy Days* when Fonzie ski-jumped over a shark, starting the show's inexorable downward spiral, this brilliant site is dedicated to documenting the moment when your favourite programme goes south. Signals of impending doom include same-character-different-actor, puberty, "A very special..." and the presence of Ted McGinley (aka Jefferson on *Married With Children*).

Like Television
www.liketelevision.com
The broadband-enabled can watch episodes of classic TV like *I Dream Of Jeannie*, *The Three Stooges* and *Bugs Bunny*.

Live TV
www.comfm.fr/live/tv
Tune into live video feeds from hundreds of real-world television stations. To record US cable shows and play them back in RealVideo (court case pending) see:
www.snapstream.com

television

With big media companies like Carlton and Granada dominating ITV, the halcyon days of regional broadcasting are almost gone. However, since television breeds lunacy like no other medium, there are a number of enthusiasts throughout the country dedicated to preserving the memory of low production values, terrible clothes and hopeless segues.

Border Television Area www.bordertvarea.co.uk
Harlech House of Graphics www.hhg.org.uk
ITV Southern England http://members.tripod.co.uk/Southern_TV
Television Southwest www.televisionsouthwest.com
Tyne Tees Logo Page www.ttlp.org.uk

Sitcoms Online
www.sitcomsonline.com
Very US-focused, but if you're looking for any information on a Yankee comedy, this is the first place to look. There are also games, discussions and polls that are fun for any comedy enthusiast regardless of nationality.

Soap City
www.soapcity.com
Keep up with who's doing what to whom, who they told and who shouldn't find out in the surreal world of soap fiction.

Test Card Circle
www.testcardcircle.org.uk
The homepage of Test Card Circle, an organization of enthusiasts of the music that accompanied the test card sequences that reigned over British TV in the dark days before cable.

The 30 Second Candidate
www.pbs.org/30secondcandidate
A fascinating history of the political TV spot from PBS, America's answer to the BBC.

Transdiffusion
www.transdiffusion.org
A truly fantastic resource for anyone interested in the history of British broadcasting, this site hosts the archives of the Transdiffusion Organization, which is dedicated to preserving the history of radio and TV in the UK. Included are screen grabs from TV coverage of historical moments, jingles, theme tunes, in-depth articles and course notes for students and teachers.

TV Eyes
www.tveyes.com
Informs you when your search term is mentioned on TV.

TV Go Home
www.tvgohome.com
Onion-style parodies of *the Radio Times*.

TV Party
www.tvparty.com
Irreverent, hilarious and more fun than a barrel of Keith Chegwins, this American site is the hall of fame that the medium truly deserves. Included are an amazing archive of uncensored out-takes, frighteningly in-depth articles about all manner of televisual ephemera and pull-no-punches features on programmes.

TV Tickets
www.tvtickets.com
Secure your chance to clap on cue.

VCR Repair Instructions
www.fixer.com
How to take a VCR apart and then get all the little bits back in so it fits more easily into the bin.

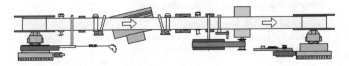

television

Virtue TV
www.virtuetv.com
If you're one of the lucky few with broadband access, this virtual channel features independent short films, an archive of music concerts and sports footage, and classic movies such as Roger Corman's *Little Shop of Horrors* and Buster Keaton's *Steamboat Bill Jr.*

WWITV
http://wwitv.com
Watch TV stations from around the world, mostly obscure.

Programme fan sites

The Web would be nothing without people who have obsessions that transcend rational thought, and television is particularly well served by fanaticism. Here are some of the best sites devoted to a single show.

Angelic Slayer www.angelicslayer.com
Run by a teenage fan from Arizona, this rather amazing site devoted to *Buffy The Vampire Slayer* and *Angel* has attracted over two million hits.

Corrie Net www.corrie.net
This *Coronation Street* archive has everything everyone could ever want to know about Ken Barlow and Hilda Ogden.

ER www.nbc.com/ER
Romance, blood and lots of helicopter crashes – what more could you want from a medical drama. If you aren't a fan of the show, you might enjoy: www.digiserve.com/er

Erinsborough.com www.erinsborough.com
Catch up with all the gossip from Ramsay Street.

Frank Butcher's Philosophical Car Lot
http://geocities.com/SunsetStrip/Stadium/1123/page1.html
RealAudio clips of *EastEnders'* philosopher-king.

Friends Place www.friendsplace.com
Every script of every episode ever. But if you have that much spare time it might make you wish you had some of your own.

Time

Calendarzone
www.calendarzone.com
Calendar links and, believe it or not, calzone recipes.

DateReminder
www.datereminder.co.uk
Remind yourself by email.

The Death Clock
www.deathclock.com
Get ready to book your final taxi.

Horology – The Index
www.horology.com
This text-heavy portal to all things pertaining to the science of
time keeping includes information on collecting timepieces, email
addresses of "cyber-horologists" and links to horological organizations.

time

International Earth Rotation Service
http://hpiers.obspm.fr
Ever felt like your bed's spinning? The truth is even scarier.

iPing (US)
www.iping.com
Arrange free telephone reminders for one or many.

Metric Time
www.billcollins.com.au/bc/mt
Decimalized excuses for being late.

Online Planners
www.supercalendar.com
Maintain your planner online. Excite, Yahoo!, MSN, and Netscape
offer similar things.

Time and Date
www.timeanddate.com
Instantly tell the time in your choice of cities. Keep your PC clock
aligned with a time synchronizer:
www.ntp.org

Time Cave
www.timecave.com
Schedule an email to be sent at a specific time in the future.

US National Debt Clock
http://brillig.com/debt_clock
Watch your children's future slip away.

USNO Master Clock Time
http://tycho.usno.navy.mil/what.html
Compute the local apparent sidereal time in your part of the world
or listen to a live broadcast of the USNO Master Clock announcer.
Get your computer's clock set by modem at:
http://tycho.usno.navy.mil/modem_time.html

Trains

End of the Line
www.wnxx.com
Site devoted to the faded (and rusting) glory of withdrawn locomotives lying on the scrap heap.

The Man in Seat 61
www.seat61.com
A superb resource – how to get from London to anywhere in the world by train (and the occasional boat).

Network Rail
www.networkrail.co.uk
Depress yourself at the state of the country's railways. To book tickets online try The Train Line or Q Jump, and for general public transport see Public Transport Info:
www.thetrainline.com
www.qjump.co.uk
www.pti.org.uk

Rail Britain
www.railbritain.com
A big site aimed at both the traveller and the enthusiast. For British rail history, see:
www.trackbed.com

Steam Locomotive
www.steamlocomotive.com
A storehouse of information on steam trains geared towards the serious, tech-minded enthusiast. Also see:
www.uksteam.info
www.steamcentral.com

Train Web
www.trainweb.org
This portal is a trainspotter's paradise. Train Web hosts chat rooms, forums, photo collections and the ever-popular Railcams.

Travel

Whether you're seeking inspiration, planning an itinerary, shopping for a ticket or already mobile, there'll be a tool online worth throwing in your box. You can book flights, reserve hotel rooms, research your destination, monitor the weather, convert currencies, learn the lingo, locate an ATM, find a restaurant that suits your fussy tastes and plenty more. For detailed listings, buy a copy of the *Rough Guide to Travel Online*. If you'd like to find first-hand experiences or travelling companions, hit the **Usenet** discussion archives at **Google** (http://groups.google.com) and join the appropriate newsgroup under the rec.travel or soc.culture hierarchies. As with all newsgroups, before you post a question, skim through the FAQs first:

Rec.Travel Library www.travel-library.com

Then see what the major guidebook publishers have to offer:

Fodors www.fodors.com
Frommer's www.frommers.com
Insiders www.insiders.com
Let's Go www.letsgo.com
Lonely Planet www.lonelyplanet.com
Moon Travel www.moon.com
Robert Young Pelton www.comebackalive.com
Rough Guides www.roughguides.com
Rough Guides Directions www.directionsguides.com
Routard www.club-internet.fr/routard

Alternatively, check out online guides such as:

CityVox www.cityvox.com
IExplore www.iexplore.com
World Travel Guide www.wtg-online.com

While it might seem like commercial suicide for the Rough Guides to give away the full text of its guides to more than ten thousand destinations, the reality is that books are still more convenient, especially on the road when you need them most. If you'd like to order a guide or map online you'll also find plenty of opportunities either from the above publishers, the online bookshops (p.47), or from travel bookshops such as:

Adventurous Traveler http://atb.away.com
Stanfords www.stanfords.co.uk

Many online travel agents also provide destination guides, which might include exclusive editorial peppered with chunks licensed from guidebooks linked out to further material on the Web. For example:

Away.com http://away.com

The biggest problem with browsing the Web for regional information and travel tools is not in finding the sites, but wading through them. Take the following directories, for example:

About Travel http://travel.about.com
Budget Travel www.budgettravel.com
Excite Travel http://travel.excite.com
Lycos Travel http://travel.lycos.com
Open Directory http://dmoz.org/Recreation/Travel
My Travel Guide www.mytravelguide.com
Traveller Online www.travelleronline.com
Virtual Tourist www.vtourist.com
World Travel Guide www.travel-guide.com
World Travel Net www.world-travel-net.com
Yahoo! Directory www.yahoo.com/Recreation/Travel
Yahoo! Travel http://travel.yahoo.com

These are perfect if you want to browse through regions look-ing for ideas, or find a range of sites on one topic – health, for example. But if you're after something very specific, you might find it more efficient to use a search engine such as **Google**. Keep adding search terms until you restrict the number of results to something manageable. If you'd like your vacation to coincide with a festival or event, go straight to:

What's on When www.whatsonwhen.com

Or for entertainment, eating, and cultural events, a city guide:

Citysearch www.citysearch.com
Time Out www.timeout.co.uk
Wcities.com www.wcities.com
Yahoo! Local http://local.yahoo.com
Zagat (Dining) www.zagat.com

If you're flexible, you might find a last-minute special. These Net exclusives are normally offered directly from the airline, hotel, and travel operator sites, which you'll find through **Yahoo!** There are also a few Web operators that specialize in late-notice and special Internet deals on flights, hotels, and so forth, such as:

Bargain Holidays www.bargainholidays.com
Best Fares www.bestfares.com
Lastminute.com www.lastminute.com
Lastminutetravel.com www.lastminutetravel.com
Opodo www.opodo.co.uk
Smarter Living www.smarterliving.com
Travel Zoo www.travelzoo.com

Booking a flight online isn't too hard, but bargains are few. Unless you're spending someone else's money you'll want to sidestep the full fares offered on these major services:

Expedia www.expedia.co.uk
Travelocity www.travelocity.co.uk
Travel Select www.travelselect.co.uk

Although they list hundreds of airlines and millions of fares, the general consensus is that they're usually better for research, accommodation and travel tips than cheap fares and customer service. So if you think it's worth the effort, drop in and check which carriers haul your route, offer the best deals and still have seats available. You can then use their rates as a benchmark. Compare them with the fares on the airline sites and discount specialists such as:

Bargain Holidays www.bargainholidays.com
Cheap Flights www.cheapflights.com
Deckchair www.deckchair.com
EasyJet www.easyjet.com
Ebookers.com www.ebookers.com
Flight Centre www.flightcentre.com
OneTravel.com www.onetravel.com
Ryanair www.ryanair.com

Or compare the prices across several agencies simultaneously, using these sites:

Farechase www.farechase.com
Hotwire www.hotwire.com
QIXO www.qixo.com
Sidestep www.sidestep.com

Finally, see if your travel agent can better the price. If the difference is only marginal, favour your agent. Then at least you'll have a human contact if something goes wrong.

travel

A2Btravel.com
www.a2btravel.com
Resources for getting into, around, and out of the UK, such as car-rental comparison, airport guides, train timetables and ferry booking.
www.ferrybooker.com
www.webweekends.co.uk

The Africa Guide
www.africaguide.com
Good, general guides of a region that nearly all the major guide books and travel services ignore. Try also:
www.africanet.com

Art of Travel
www.artoftravel.com
How to see the world on $25 a day.

ATM Locators
www.visa.com/atms
Locate a hole in the wall willing to replenish your wallet. Also try:
www.mastercard.comcardholderservices/atm

Backpacker.com
www.backpacker.com
Excellent site for wilderness trekkers, including destination guides, tips on keeping your boots in shape and the real dope on DEET-free insect repellents.

The Bathroom Diaries
www.thebathroomdiaries.com
One of the most essential sites on the Web: You're in Bamako, Mali, when nature calls and you're after a good, clean Western-style toilet, click here to find out the nearest one.

Bed & Breakfast.com
www.bedandbreakfast.com
Secure a good night's sleep worldwide.
www.bedandbreakfast-directory.co.uk
www.babs.com.au
www.innsite.com

Bugbog
www.bugbog.co.uk
Nice, compact, easy-to-navigate mini-guides for people wanting to go somewhere a bit out of the ordinary. Good features include the best beaches in the world by month, and a destination finder giving you options such as colourful culture, festivals and weather.

Caravan Sitefinder
http://caravan-sitefinder.co.uk
Where to hitch your rusting hulk of steel without looking like hippy scum. For places to pitch your tent, try Camp Sites:
www.camp-sites.co.uk

CIA World Factbook
www.cia.gov/cia/publications/factbook
Vital stats on every country. For the score on living standards:
www.undp.org

Danger Finder
www.comebackalive.com/df
Adventure holidays that could last a lifetime.

Electronic Embassy
www.embassy.org
Directory of foreign embassies in DC plus Web links where available. Search Yahoo! for representation in other cities.

travel

Family Travel Files
www.thefamilytravelfiles.com
Look here for help on what to do when the little monsters start asking, "Are we there yet?" For more UK-specific destinations, try Planit4Kids:
www.planit4kids.com

Flight Arrivals & Departures
www.flightarrivals.com
Stay on top of takeoffs and touchdowns across North America.

Gap Year
www.gapyear.com
Excellent site dedicated to students about to take a year out, with loads of travel tips and stories.

Global Freeloaders
www.globalfreeloaders.com
Take in a globetrotting dosser.

Hotel Discount
www.hoteldiscount.com
Book hotels around the world. For backpacker rates, try:
www.hostels.com

How far is it?
www.indo.com/distance
Calculate the distance between any two cities.

IgoUgo
www.igougo.com
Packed full of travellers' photos and journals, this roughguides.com partner site offers candid first-hand information.

International Home Exchange Network
www.homexchange.com
Trade your dreary digs for a palatial beach house. More here:
www.sunswap.com
www.homebase-hols.com

International Student Travel Confederation
www.istc.org
Save money with an authentic international student card.

Journeywoman
www.journeywoman.com
Reporting in from the sister beaten track.

OAG
www.oag.com
Largest database of flight schedules on the Net, which can be down-
loaded to your Palm or mobile.

The Original Tipping Page
www.tipping.org
Make fast friends with the bell-hop.

Resorts Online
www.resortsonline.com
Your way through three thousand resorts throughout the world cat-
egorized by beach, golf, spa, ski, etc.

Roadside America
www.roadsideamerica.com
Strange attractions on US highways.

Sahara Overland
www.sahara-overland.com
Leave the city in a cloud of dust.

Subway Navigator
www.subwaynavigator.com
Estimate the travelling times between city stations worldwide.

Theme Parks of England
http://themeparksofengland.com
Reviews and info on all the major high G-force thrills to be had without leaving the country.

travel

Tips4Trips
www.tips4trips.com
More than a thousand tips for the traveller, from packing to navigating Customs on your way back home.

TNT Live!
www.tntmagazine.com
Survive London and venture onward with aid from expat streetmags, *TNT* and *Southern Cross*.

Tourism Offices Worldwide
www.towd.com
Write to the local tourist office. They might send you a brochure. For even more propaganda, try Official Travel Info:
www.officialtravelinfo.com

Traffic and Road Conditions
www.accutraffic.com
Live traffic and weather updates. Also to be found here:
www.rac.co.uk/check_traffic/?view=Standard&nav

Traffic Signs of the World
www.elve.net/rcoulst.htm
Next time you're in Kyrgyzstan, you'll know when to look out for the men at work.

Travelmag
www.travelmag.co.uk
Several intimate travel reflections monthly.

Travel Paperwork
www.travelpaperwork.com
Sort out the red tape before you hit the border.

Unclaimed Baggage
www.unclaimedbaggage.com
You lose it; they sell it.

Travel health online

Don't ignore medical bulletins if you're planning to visit a potential hotspot or health risk, but seek a second opinion before postponing your adventure.

Foreign Office www.fco.gov.uk
Australian Government www.dfat.gov.au
US State Department http://travel.state.gov

Also take a look at these useful sites:

Rough Guide to Travel Health http://travel.roughguides.com/health
Masta www.masta.org
Travel Doctor www.tmvc.com.au
TravelHealth.com www.travelhealth.co.uk
World Health Organization www.who.int

Then brace yourself against the bugs eagerly awaiting your arrival. For a list of travel medicine clinics worldwide, see:

Travel Health Online www.tripprep.com

UK Passport Agency
www.ukpa.gov.uk
Speed up your passport application at this streamlined site.

Underbelly
www.underbelly.com
Short, sharp, shocked guides to the places tourists rarely ever see.

Universal Currency Converter
www.xe.com/ucc
Convert Finnish markkas into Central African francs on the fly. More at Oanda:
www.oanda.com

Vindigo
www.vindigo.com
Is Vindigo the future of travel guides? Download its Palm Pilot or AvantGo city guides and decide for yourself.

webcams

Virtual Tourist
www.virtualtourist.com
Big database of travel reviews written by ordinary people, not travel journalists on press junkets. The reviews are hooked up to maps and links to other sites.

Walkabout
www.walkabout.com.au
Get the lowdown on the land down under.

WebFlyer
www.webflyer.com
Keep tabs on frequent flyer schemes.

What's On When?
www.whatsonwhen.com
Annoyed you've missed Thaipusam or the turning of the bones yet again? Get your dates right here.

World Heritage Listing
www.unesco.org/whc
Plan your itinerary around international treasures.

World Travel Tips
www.worldtraveltips.net
A good, all-round destination site; the layout is clear, maps are good, and there are Yahoo! links for news headlines of each destination.

Webcams

Africam
www.africam.com
Go on a (virtual) safari without even leaving your armchair.

The Amazing Cooler Cam
www.coolercam.com
As if your workplace wasn't boring enough, watch Americans get

drinks from the office water cooler.

Beer Lover Cam
www.beerlovercam.com
Watch a couple of guys agonize over whether to grab a can of Bud or just go for the Miller.

Earth Cam
www.earthcam.com
Links to a vast array of webcams, usefully organized into categories and subcategories including Traffic, Arts & Entertainment, Metro, Weird and more. Also check Webcam Central and Webcam World:
www.camcentral.com
www.webcamworld.com

Fly on the Wall
www.flyonthewall.com
A portal dedicated to webcams and streaming video footage of movie premieres and showbiz parties, as well as Times Square, spacecraft landings and, umm, guinea pigs.

Mount St Helens VolcanoCam
http://www.fs.fed.us/gpnf/volcanocams/msh
Don't hold your breath.

Pavement Terror
www.backfire.co.uk
As if you needed more reason not to trust White Van Man, former delivery man Howard Stone has posted streaming videos of pedestrian horror when his van backfires.

Steve's Ant Farm
www.stevesantfarm.com
Watch blurry black punctuation marks build tunnels.

Wearcam
www.wearcam.org
Your one-stop shop for information on "photoborgs" and wearable computers.

Weird

Absurd.org
www.absurd.org
Please do not adjust your set.

Aliens In The Bible
http://aliensinthebible.com
Fact: spooky space dudes are stealing our souls. The Bible wouldn't lie about something that important. If you think you may be an alien (not necessarily in the Bible), see the Alien Counsel at:
www.angelfire.com/md/aliencounsel

American Pie and the Armageddon Prophecy
www.roytaylorministries.com
How Madonna testified against the descendants of Israel all the way to number one. But what tragedy awaits her:
www.geocities.com/Athens/Atrium/3933/madonna.htm

Animal Mating Zone
www.matings.co.uk
Hardcore sex: the type you only get to see in wildlife documentaries.

Entrances To Hell
www.entrances2hell.co.uk
Damnation is to be found in the strangest of places.

Christian Guide to Small Arms
www.frii.com/~gosplow/cgsa.html
"He that hath no sword, let him sell his garment and buy one" – Luke 22:36. It's not just your right; it's your duty, darnit.

Circlemakers
www.circlemakers.org
Create crop circles to amuse New Agers and the press.

A Citizen from Hell
www.amightywind.com/hell/citizenhell.htm
If Hell sounds this bad, you don't want to go there.

Borgstrom.com
www.borgstrom.com
Hours of fun hitting a man with a beard around the face with your mouse pointer.

Clonaid
www.clonaid.com
Thanks to the Raelians, we now know all life on earth was created in extraterrestrial laboratories. Here's where you can buy genuine cloned human livestock for the kitchen table. Ready as soon as the lab's finished.

Corpses for Sale
http://distefano.com
Brighten up your guestroom with a life-sized chew-toy.

Corrugated Iron Club
www.corrugated-iron-club.info
It's metal. It's wavy. It rocks.

The Darwin Awards
www.darwinawards.com
Each year the Darwin Award goes to the person who drops off the census register in the most spectacular fashion. Here's where to read about the runners-up and er ... winners.

Deep Black Magic
www.mindspring.com/~txporter
Forty years of CIA research into mind control and ESP. For the perspective of a Finnish immigrant to Canada on mind control, see: http://hackcanada.com/canadian/freedom/mylife.html

Derm Cinema
www.skinema.com
Know your celebrity skin conditions.

weird

Dr MegaVolt
www.drmegavolt.com
The Doc sure sparked right up when they switched on the power,
but could he cut it in the big league?
www3.bc.sympatico.ca/lightningsurvivor

English Rose Press
www.englishrosepress.com
Diana sends her love from Heaven.

Fetish Map
www.deviantdesires.com/map/map.html
Join the dots between piggy-players, fursuiters, inflators, crush
freaks and where you're standing now.

Flatulence Filter
http://flatulence-filter.com
Because life wasn't meant to be a gas.

Fortean Times
www.forteantimes.com
Updates from the print monthly that takes the investigation of
strange phenomena more seriously than itself. See also:
www.bizarremag.com

Future Horizons
www.futurehorizons.net
Snap off more than your fair share through solid-state circuitry.

God Channel
www.godchannel.com
Relay requests to God via His official Internet channel.

Gum Blondes
www.gumblondes.com
Portraits of your favourite blondes lovingly fashioned from chewed bubblegum.

Great Joy In Great Tribulation
www.dccsa.com/greatjoy
Biblical proof that Prince Chuck is the Antichrist and key dates leading to the end of the world. For more enlightenment, including how to debug the pyramids, see:
www.bibleprophecy.net

I Can Eat Glass Project
www.geocities.com/nodotus/hbglass.html
Deter excess foreign suitors and carpet dealers with the only words you know in their language.

Illuminati News
www.illuminati-news.com
Storm into secret societies and thump your fist on the table.

International Ghost Hunters Society
www.ghostweb.com
They never give up the ghost. Nab your own with:
www.ghostresearch.org
www.maui.net/~emf/TriFieldNat.html

Itz Fun Tew Be Dat Kandie Kid
www.angelfire.com/ma/talulaQ/kandie.html
Mothers – don't let your babies grow up to be ravers.

weird

Lego Death
www.thefrown.com/blockdeath
Unpleasant death scenes from the guillotine to Elvis dying on the crapper rendered with block toys. For Bible stories illustrated with plastic blocks, go to:
www.thereverend.com/brick_testament

A Mathematical Survey of the English Language
www.geocities.com/garywaterbury
Plot your future through simple arithmetic.

Mozart's Musikalisches Würfelspeil
http://sunsite.univie.ac.at/Mozart/dice
Compose a minuet as you play Monopoly.

Mudboy
www.mudboyuk.com
Some get their kicks from muddy boots.

Museum of Non-Primate Art
www.monpa.com
Become an aficionado of moggy masterpieces.

Neuticles
www.neuticles.com
Pick your pet's pocket but leave his dignity intact.

News of the Weird
www.newsoftheweird.com
www.thisistrue.com
www.weirdlist.com
Dotty clippings from the world press.

Nibiruan Council
www.nibiruancouncil.com
Stock your bar to welcome the heroic Starseeds, Walkins, and Lightworkers from the Battlestar Nibiru, who will finally usher in the fifth dimensional reality.

Nobody Here
www.nobodyhere.com
Sometimes things with the least purpose are the most enthralling.

Non-escalating Verbal Self Defence
www.taxi1010.com
Fight insults by acting insane.

The Ozone Cow
http://theozonecow.cjb.net
The story of the two most unsuccessful children's book writers in history, ever.

PhobiaList
http://phobialist.com
So much to fear, it's scary.

Planetary Activation Organization
www.paoweb.com
Prevent inter-dimensional dark forces from dominating our galaxy by ganging up with the Galactic Federation of Light.

Professional Paranoid
www.proparanoid.com
For when nobody else will believe you.

weird

Reincarnation.org
www.reincarnation-org.com
Stash your loot with this crowd, then come back to collect it in your next life.

Reptoids
www.reptoids.com
Was that an alien or merely the subterranean descendant of a dinosaur?

The Republic of Texas Provisional Government
www.republic-of-texas.net
Rednecks for liberty, fraternity and equality.

The Sacred Geometry Stories of Jesus Christ
www.jesus8880.com
How to decode the big J's mathematical word puzzle.

Sightings
www.rense.com
Fishy newsbreaks from talk-radio truth ferret Jeff Rense.

Streakerama
www.streakerama.com
Get to the bottom of the streaker phenomenon.

Sulabh International Museum of Toilets
www.sulabhtoiletmuseum.org
Follow the evolution of the ablution at the world's leading exhibition of bathroom businessware. No need to take it sitting down: www.restrooms.org

Terry J. Hokanson Lives Under the Mafia
www.geocities.com/terry_tune
Mild-mannered inventor speaks out against the crime syndicate that controls his life through government hypnotists.

Time Travellers
http://time-travelers.org
Step back to a time that common sense forgot.

Toe Amputation Project

www.bme.freeq.com/spc/toecutter.htm

No big deal. He still has one left.

Toilet-train Your Cat

www.karawynn.net/mishacat

How to point pusskins at the porcelain.

Trapped Angels

www.cyberspaceorbit.com/april.html

Leading authorities point to evidence that angels may be alien frauds.

The Twinkies Project

www.twinkiesproject.com

Only here can you find out what happens to a Twinkie when you drop it from a great height or expose it to radiation, and then read the results of such experiments in haiku form.

weird

Why I will never have a girlfriend
www.nothingisreal.com/girlfriend
Derived from first principles, and confirmed by his nickname.

World Database of Happiness
www.eur.nl/fsw/research/happiness
Discover where people are happiest.

Xenophobic Persecution in the UK
www.five.org.uk
If you're below British standards, the MI5 will punish you by TV.

Yellow Snow
http://pi.pwp.blueyonder.co.uk/snow.html
It's better than pissing into the wind.

ZetaTalk
www.zetatalk.com
Nancy's guests today are those elusive aliens that frolic in the autumn mist at the bottom of her garden.